Motivating At-Risk Students

Mary Riordan Karlsson, M.A.

Teacher Created Materials, Inc.

Cover Design by Darlene Spivak

Made in U.S.A.

ISBN 1-55734-890-1

Order Number TCM 890

Table of Contents

Introduction

Professional's Guide: Motivating At-Risk Learners discusses the concept of motivation and examines the many factors that influence an at-risk learner in the classroom learning environment. Chapters highlight such topics as identifying at-risk learners, various motivational theories, personal and cognitive influencing factors, creating a positive classroom environment that provides motivational opportunities, instructional strategies which will encourage at-risk learners to become engaged in various literacy tasks, assessment practices, and ideas that teachers can share with parents to motivate at-risk learners at home. Throughout the chapters, examples across the curriculum are provided to support the ideas and perspectives of the motivational theories in the classroom and at home. Sample literacy activities are also included to help you begin to think about setting up your classroom to be a positive learning environment for children who are at risk.

I emphasize reading and writing since they are key elements to success in all content areas and give you many ideas on how to engage your at-risk learners in various literacy tasks, including social studies, math, and science hands-on activities that will motivate them to want to learn.

As you read this book, I hope you will begin to understand more clearly the concept of motivation and the various internal and external factors that influence a learner's motivation, attitude, and desire to learn. *Motivating At-Risk Learners* offers you the opportunity to reflect on the teaching and learning process and strategies for enhancing the educational experience for at-risk learners.

Identifying At-Risk Learners

Who Is at Risk?

When you think about the students in your class and try to decide who is at risk, specific students will come to mind. This learner is a low achiever who has difficulty with reading and writing and is, therefore, at risk of experiencing failure, frustration, and retention. This learner tends to devalue reading and writing for subcultural reasons (i.e., peer group) or because of personal frustrations previously experienced with language arts, math, social studies, or science.

Students can be at risk due to academic, social, emotional, or economic reasons. The U.S. Government Accounting Office Report (1993) states that, "poor children are more likely than non-poor children to be in at-risk categories. To succeed in school, these children often need special help that may or may not be available, such as language or family support services" (p. 6). Many children in the at-risk categories lack experiences with literacy, as well as the encouragement and support from their families; thus, they come to school looking for just that. They need more time and opportunities to participate in literacy activities to build their self-esteem and develop posi-

> **Students can be at risk due to academic, social, emotional, or economic reasons.**

1

tive attitudes towards learning. Therefore, it is very important that your classroom offers appropriate literacy activities which include reading and writing tasks in all content areas that will motivate them to want to learn.

Motivating at-risk learners to become engaged in literacy tasks across the curriculum is a challenge for many teachers. This requires not only creating a learning environment which encourages reading, writing, drawing, computing, experimenting, and discussing ideas, but it also requires you to tap into the student's affective and cognitive domains to engage the student in these tasks in all of the content areas, including science, math, and social studies, as well as the fine arts.

Motivating at-risk learners to become engaged in literacy tasks across the curriculum is a challenge for many teachers.

Additionally, it is important for you to be aware of the personal factors students bring with them, which can play a major role in the learning process and have a positive or negative influence on the student's intention or desire to read, write, or learn. Therefore, these factors must also be identified and examined in detail to help you plan lessons and units that will motivate at-risk learners. We all want to reach out to each and every student in our class, but the only way to do this successfully is to understand where these students are coming from and whether they have a past history of success or failure.

A Resurgence of Interest in Motivational Issues

In the 1980s, there was a resurgence of interest in motivational issues among researchers and teachers in the field of reading and writing. The role of the teachers was changing; not only were they expected to teach subject matter but also to teach the desire to learn as well. Developing the motivation to read, write, or learn within the classroom and encouraging students to do the same outside the classroom, for both academic and personal reasons, became a concern for teachers and reading specialists and is still a concern today.

For example, in a recent poll done by the International Reading Association, its members, mostly teachers and reading specialists, elected "creating interest in reading" as the top priority for research. Other priorities in the top 10 included studying intrinsic desire for reading and increasing students' amount and breadth of reading (Guthrie, 1994). This is telling us that student engagement in reading is a must and that we need to look at the factors that influence a reader's intention to read as well as write, compute, and experiment in the classroom learning environment. If learners are unmotivated to read and write in any content area, they are missing out on an essential element in the learning process.

It appears that a contributing factor to the low interest in reading may be the amount of time a child spends watching television. It has been found that reading from books occupies less than 1% of a child's free time in contrast to an average of 130 minutes of television viewing per day (Anderson, Wilson, & Fielding, 1985).

The above findings highlight for us the importance of the development of motivation to learn and increasing student engagement in literacy activities across the curriculum. Despite studies conducted for the recent National Assessment of Educational Progress 1992 Reading Report Card for the Nation and the States (Mullis, Campbell, & Farstrup, 1993; Applebee, Langer, and Mullis, 1988) which have shown that students who read most read best. More and more children would rather watch television than read a book or play a video game instead of doing a crossword puzzle. The Reading Report Card, 1971–1988, (Mullis & Jenkins, 1990) indicates that while students are required to read more often as they progress through the grades, they engage in less independent pleasure reading. Many students clearly just lack the motivation or the intention to read in any or all of the content areas. It is important to remember how much reading is required in science, math, social studies, health, art, and even music. Thus, we must encourage our students to read a variety of texts and engage in a variety of tasks.

A student's motivation to learn and interest in reading, writing, math, science, and social studies may remain low if many classrooms are not positive learning environments.

Why Do We Need to Address These Issues?

We need to address these issues because we are witnessing a decline in motivation to learn. Perhaps reading is not fun because it is a struggle or a chore, especially for at-risk learners. Literacy activities have stiff competition, such as television, computers, videos, and CDs. We are discovering that children are not intrinsically motivated to read, write, or learn; instead, they choose to passively use their minds to watch MTV or a video and are thus, contributing to the widespread literacy problem in the United States. Unfortunately, we have become a society of people who can read and write but simply are not inclined to do so. To use Hynds' (1990) term, the literacy problem in the United States is to a great extent one of "alliteracy," people who can read and write but choose not to. This is a problem in many classrooms across the country; therefore, it is an issue we must address.

A student's motivation to learn and interest in reading, writing, math, science, and social studies may remain low if their classrooms are not positive learning environments. Efforts need to be taken to design instructional learning environments that will ignite students' interests and create a sense of desire to engage in literacy tasks. Through these engaging literacy tasks, students will develop intrinsic motivation and positive attitudes toward learning at an early age that can be sustained throughout their lifetimes. Participants in these activities can include teachers, cross-age reading buddies, parents, and other literate adults who can act as role models, such as local athletes (Riordan, 1992).

Identifying the Influencing Factors

It is necessary to identify the various personal and social factors that influence a learner's intention to learn because without intention or desire, the learner will not experience the challenge and pleasure of the learning process. Also, it is important for teachers to be aware of these various factors so they can integrate them into instructional strategies and literacy development activities in the classroom learning environment.

At-risk students enjoy learning when they are able to socially construct meanings and ideas.

Motivating skilled readers and writers is not as difficult because they have developed intrinsic (internal) motivation to engage in these tasks. These students have already received positive rewards from engaging in these tasks (such as, good grades, stickers, positive report cards, special privileges in class). However, at-risk students need extra incentives to engage themselves in these tasks again. These students who are at risk of experiencing failure need both an inviting classroom context and some personal incentives or intrinsic motivations to engage in various reading and writing tasks in all content areas.

Concluding Remarks

I have taken a sociocognitive perspective on learning; therefore, I will examine both the social factors (within the classroom learning environment) and cognitive factors (within the reader's head). Additionally, I am looking through a social constructivist lens, grounded in Vygotsky's (1978) work which believes that children learn through social interaction and construct meaning through these interactions. Based on recent research, it appears that students appreciate working with others, sharing knowledge, and constructing new meanings through dialogue and social activities. At-risk students enjoy learning when they are able to socially construct meanings and ideas. This notion of learning through interaction is also derived from John Dewey's (1938) work as he emphasizes that children learn through experiences using the "hands-on" approach. This will be a main theme throughout and will be explicit in the instructional strategies and assessment practices that you can implement in your own classroom.

Overview of Motivational Theories

Questions About Motivation

Why are some learners motivated and others are not? This is a question which is commonly asked by teachers and parents alike. Motivation is a difficult term to define; instead, it is easier to describe it according to behavior. For example, a student who is motivated to engage in literacy tasks will take the initiative and choose to read a book, write a story, play with math manipulatives, or conduct a science experiment during free time. Less motivated students will choose to play and shy away from the "academic" literacy tasks, which include reading, writing, or computing. This is normal behavior for these students who have previously had negative experiences and have become quite frustrated with themselves because they cannot read, understand, or spell some words,.

Children are very perceptive and competitive; they are aware of what their friends, siblings, and classmates can do and what they cannot do. Therefore, at-risk students will choose activities they have previously been successful with and know they will not be frustrated. Thus, the challenge remains; how can teachers motivate these at-risk

Children are very perceptive and competitive; they are aware of what their friends, siblings, and classmates can do and what they cannot do.

students to engage in various literacy tasks across the curriculum? The answer to this question is not a quick and easy one. The first step is to clarify and understand some theories and ideas about motivation, and then apply them to the classroom. It is very important for teachers and parents to be clear on the concept of what motivation is; then, you can decide how to motivate your students/children both in the classroom and at home.

Understanding Motivation

Motivation is an area that is taken for granted. Naturally, the assumption is that all students are motivated to learn and want to read and write and participate in all of the wonderful activities that you plan. However, this is not always the case. There usually is an underlying reason why a student does not want to participate; he/she is simply not motivated to do so. Therefore, it is important for teachers and parents to understand what it actually means when a child is not motivated or lacks the desire to participate.

Even though motivation is a difficult concept to define, it is a very important one to understand since it is an essential element in the learning process.

Even though motivation is a difficult concept to define, it is a very important one to understand since it is an essential element in the learning process. As Marty Covington (1992), a psychologist who has been extensively researching the area of motivation, says, "Motivation, like the concept of gravity, is easier to describe (in terms of its outward, observable effects) than it is to define" (p.1). He explains the discrepancy of motivation by stating, "Knowing how to motivate is not the same as knowing what is motivation" (p.1). In the realm of reader motivation, Mathewson (1994) defines motivation as the development of conditions promoting intention to read. And he defines intention as the mediator between attitude and reading. Intention is more than this; it is creating the desire or the decision to read. This theory can be applied to any literacy activity across the content areas. If the intention or desire is not present, a child will decide not to participate in the activity or task or will not participate in a meaningful way.

Although there has recently been a resurgence of interest in motivational theory as psychologists try to apply the findings of cognitive psychology to fields such as education, there still remains a lack of research in the area of motivation in reading, writing, math, and science. Consequently, we need to apply general motivational theories of learning to better understand these processes.

A Closer Look into Motivation

When we consider motivation, we deal with the WHY of behavior (Covington 1992). Also, we must look at what individuals are motivated to do. Motivation varies in two ways, direction and intensity, and can be defined as the impact of needs and desires on the direction and intensity of an individual's behavior (Slavin, 1991). This direction and intensity influences a student's intent or decision to engage in reading and writing tasks similar to the way competence and control influence a learner's intention to learn. If a learner feels competent to complete the task and also feels in control of the task, he/she will be more motivated to engage in the task and follow through with it until completion. If a learner does not feel competent or in control, his/her frustration levels will rise, and he/she will not want to engage in the task.

Another theory that provides insight into the area of motivation and the learning process includes Maslow's (1954) needs hierarchy, which ranges from physiological needs at the base to self-actualizing needs at the pinnacle. Among the growth needs in this hierarchy is the need to know and understand, which is what naturally motivates some students. This perspective can be applied to all of the content areas. All students want to know and understand; it is just more difficult for some, but with some extra help and careful planning, learning can become easier for them.

The achievement motivation theory (McClelland, Atkinson, Clark, & Lowell, 1953) can also be applied to learning to read, write, draw, or compute. Students who are high in achievement motivation are likely to strive for success by choosing challenging goals when reading, writing, drawing, or conducting a science experiment. They may choose more challenging books and persist in the efforts necessary to complete difficult assignments. When applying this theory to at-risk students, they may have low achievement motivation and thus not strive for challenges but rather stay within their comfort zones.

Covington's (1992) "self-worth" theory is extremely relevant to at-risk learners, which posits that perceived self-worth strongly affects the degree to which the students become effective learners in the instructional setting. An important aspect of motivating at-risk learners is to provide activities that will boost their self-esteem and confidence. Typically, they have a low self-worth which is reflected in their school work. They are unwilling to take risks for fear of failure and embarrassment. Therefore, you must boost their self-worth to encourage them to become effective and motivated learners.

Motivation to read, write, compute, draw, experiment, or discover is closely connected to opportunities to experience a sense of enjoyment while engaging in the activity. To truly experience the intrinsic rewards of learning, students must achieve a balance between the difficulty of the task and their own ability. If the challenge of the task

Motivation to read, write, compute, draw, experiment, or discover is closely connected to opportunities to experience a sense of enjoyment while engaging in the activity.

is too high, the learner will experience anxiety, and, conversely, if the challenge is too low, boredom will result. More likely, the former case is typical for at-risk learners.

Two Types of Motivation: Extrinsic and Intrinsic

There are two types of motivation, extrinsic (external) and intrinsic (internal), both of which are formative parts of the learning process. External motivation is something that engages us in an activity when it is clear that by participating in it, we are likely to have a positive experience and accomplish our desired outcome. Internal motivation is characterized by a desire to engage in an activity because doing so brings personal satisfaction, regardless of potential extrinsic outcomes.

Learners need to have the confidence and competence to engage in any kind of task, be it reading, writing, math, science, social studies, art, or music.

Essentially, intrinsic motivation is the by-product of two sets of self-perceptions, those of competence and self-determination (Deci, 1975). If learners perceive themselves as being capable of completing an assignment and also feel they have some degree of control over the task or outcome, they are more likely to be intrinsically motivated to engage in that literacy event (an activity that includes reading, writing, speaking, or listening). Conversely, if either of these perceptions is not present, intrinsic motivation is also likely to be missing (Spaulding, 1992).

However, it seems likely that when perceptions of both competence and self-determination are high, intrinsic motivation is usually high as well. Learners need to have the confidence and competence to engage in any kind of task, be it reading, writing, math, science, social studies, art, or music. If the task appears to be too difficult, they will not want to do it. Therefore, it is important to instill a sense of confidence, competence, and control in learners when planning lessons across the curriculum.

Both the extrinsic and intrinsic factors promote motivation and intention to participate in any activity. The extrinsic factors include the setting, the difficulty of the material, peer pressure or peer interaction, the goal of the assignment, the teacher's instructional strategy, and the amount of time given to complete the activity and talk about it. Most of these factors are not in the student's control; however, many of the intrinsic factors can be controlled by the students, such as their own personal goals or purposes, their self-worth, self-confidence, their attitudes, and their responses to the activity. All of these factors will be discussed in detail in later chapters.

It is important to remember these intrinsic motivations when planning an activity or a unit. At-risk learners need to develop many or all of these intrinsic motivations which in turn can develop self-confidence and build their self-esteem. The development of these motivations are crucial for at-risk learners, since the external motivators may not be exciting or prove to be successful for them. If they have previously experienced failure, or poor grades, it is the internal motivators they need to rely on.

The Connection Between Motivation and Attitude

Motivation is linked very closely to attitude and vice versa, through the intention or desire a learner possesses. These three factors are dependent upon each other; think of it as a Venn diagram with three interconnecting circles with the learner in the middle. On one hand, if there is no motivation and a negative attitude, most likely, there will be no intention or desire to engage in a literacy task. On the other hand, if a student has a positive attitude, he/she will more likely be very motivated and develop the intention to engage in a literacy task. Learners need the intention or desire to learn in order to engage themselves in an activity.

Motivation is linked very closely to attitude and vice versa, through the intention or desire a learner possesses.

During any kind of activity we should encourage the learner to become involved by "pretending" to be a scientist, a mathematician, or an author. Approaching the activity from a different perspective may assist the learner. Encourage the student to take on another role; for example, during social studies have him/her pretend to be Martin Luther King, Jr. leading a Civil Rights March and write a speech for the occasion, or when conducting an experiment, have him/her pretend to be Marie Curie and try to find out more about radiology. Allowing the student to step out of his/her usual role and take on another one can develop high motivation and positive attitudes, which is one of your goals. When reading a story, encourage the reader to "step into the story," to experience and live through the story as one of the characters. At-risk learners need to be encouraged and motivated to "step into the story" and experience success more frequently. During writing activities, these internal motivations encourage the writer to also "step into the story" and identify with his/her own work and take on the persona of one of the characters or the narrator.

Other internal motivations include skill and will, which are two requirements of learning and performance and are characteristically not developed in at-risk learners. They may have the skill and not the will, or, more often than not, at-risk learners have the will but not the skill, thus creating a frustrating situation. They want to do the task but do not know how to do it and need help. Extrinsic (external) and intrinsic (internal) motives work in combination to motivate a reader to read, a writer to write, a scientist to experiment, and a mathematician to compute. Motivation is also connected to the learner's perception of the value of the learning situation and his/her ability to do well. This issue ties closely to confidence, competence, and control, which was discussed earlier and will also tie into the notion of reader responsibility which will be discussed later.

The fear of failure or fear of success may also hinder a student's motivation to participate in a literacy activity. As previously mentioned, if a student has experienced failure in reading or writing activities, he/she will be hesitant to attempt the activity again. Therefore, the fear of failure decreases the motivational drive. If they have experienced success, it is true they will be more motivated, but, surprisingly, some students possess a fear of success which means they feel pressure to always succeed, and if that pressure is too much, they will be less motivated to challenge themselves because they feel they must succeed. These two fears can easily influence a student's motivational drive.

> The fear of failure or fear of success may also hinder a student's motivation to participate in a literacy activity.

When faced with a challenge of reading or writing, the learner must evaluate the situation and make an internal decision to engage in the task; this is called intention. Usually the learner's intention is influenced by a previously formed attitude, and unfortunately for many at-risk learners, this attitude is based on prior negative experiences with reading and writing tasks in some of the different content areas. So, it is important to develop positive attitudes toward reading and writing in all of the content areas with at-risk learners. This can be done through careful planning and the identification of the various factors that influence a learner's attitude, as well as motivation, such as the personal, affective, cognitive, and social factors. These factors will be identified and discussed in the following two chapters.

Concluding Remarks

Indeed, motivation is a difficult term to define as well as describe. At-risk learners need that vote of confidence before they engage in a task, and we can give them that confidence in many ways. The various theories and ideas about motivation should be taken into consideration when designing a unit, planning lessons, and creating a learning environment in which all students, especially those at risk, can thrive in and not feel frustration and give up. It is one of the many goals of the teacher to motivate students to learn to the best of their abilities. It is easier to do this when you understand the concept of motivation and are aware of the behavioral changes that denote an increase or decrease in motivation. Once you know what motivation is, you can then concentrate on how to motivate your students.

Personal Factors
Influencing Learners

Individual Differences

Within the concept of motivation, there are various personal, affective, cognitive, and social factors that need to be identified and examined which influence and motivate a learner to engage in an activity or task. Individuals are predisposed by personal factors and their personality characteristics when approaching the reading and writing process. The personal factors are those that a student brings into the classroom, such as purposes, goals, self-worth, self-regulation, self-determination, and family values and beliefs. These factors can originate from family traditions and cultural beliefs in the home environment or in the early experiences in the school environment.

The home environment is a determining factor in a student's motivation, attitude, and achievement.

The home environment is a determining factor in a student's motivation, attitude, and achievement. It is important to focus not only on the physical surroundings of the home environment but also to look at the literacy surroundings. How does the family use literacy? What kinds of activities do the children participate in? Do the parents include the children in their conversations or other literacy activities, such as writing grocery lists, reading the newspaper, and writing notes or messages? Does the family discuss current events or watch the news on television? Do the parents explain the concept of money to the children? Who is responsible for the finances (i.e., grocery money, school clothes, telephone bill)? A student will carry with him/herself attributes of both surroundings; therefore, it is critical to identify these "hidden" personal factors that a student possesses.

Purposes and Goals

The purpose is the reason for reading, writing, computing, drawing, or creating. It is the plan which guides the learner to accomplish his/her goal. There are many different purposes or orientations for reading or conducting a science experiment. The purpose for learning can be self-regulated and self-determined or teacher-regulated and teacher-determined. It is extremely important for the learner to know the purpose for the task. Frequently, the learner is unaware of the purpose and cannot understand why he/she has to do the task, thus creating a reason not to be motivated. If the learner is clear on the purpose, the motivation level may be higher, and he/she will try harder to complete the task. And when the learner can decide what the purpose is, the motivation level will definitely increase; he/she will feel in control and have more confidence.

> It is extremely important for the learner to know the purpose for the task.

The goal of learning is an end or objective the learner sets in his/her mind. It is included within the purpose and may also be either self-regulated and self-determined or teacher-regulated and teacher-determined. A learner's goal in literacy tasks may be intrinsic, for a sense of ownership and accomplishment, natural rewards, or maybe to simply finish the task. Or the learner's goals may be extrinsic, such as grades or competition among classmates. Either way, the learner must set a purpose which drives the goal prior to the literacy event and understand that this purpose may change throughout the activity. Most at-risk learners set easy goals, ones they know they can attain, or else they lose sight of the goal as they progress through the activity or task. If they become frustrated quickly, they will abandon their original goal and just want to finish as quickly and painlessly as possible, which will only decrease their motivation level to try that same task again. It is also very important for the learner to decide or choose his/her own goal for different tasks. Once again this gives him/her a chance to be in control and build self-confidence. This is a critical component for at-risk learners.

Understanding Oneself as a Learner

A combination of self-esteem and self-confidence a learner possesses makes up a learner's self-worth. A student's perception of self-worth definitely affects the student's participation in an activity within the instructional setting. A high priority for students is to protect their self-esteem and their sense of ability. They may even handicap themselves by not studying because to try hard and fail anyway reflects poorly on their ability, and they do not want that to happen.

It is good for you to be aware of the self-esteem of your at-risk learners. In the sample Self-Esteem Survey on the next page, learners can fill this out and discuss with you some of their feelings about what they are good at, their favorite books, what activities they do and do not like, and their aspirations when they grow up, just as some examples. It is important for you to let the learner know that you care about him/her and respect his/her feelings. Also, by knowing this information, you can plan lessons which aim to build students' self-esteem in many ways.

Self-Esteem

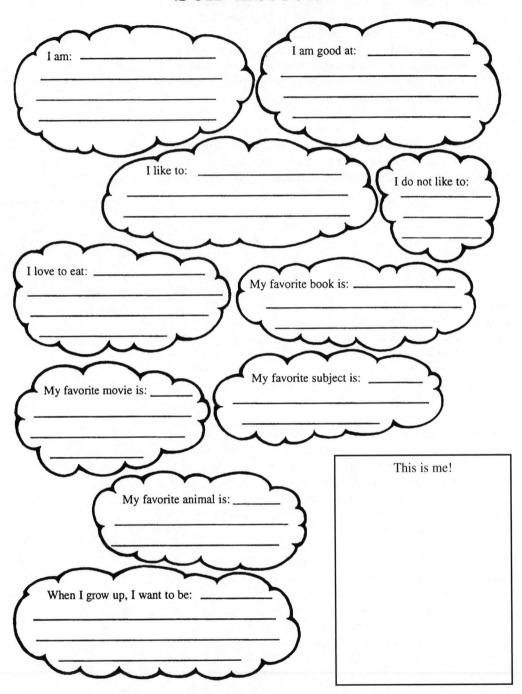

I am: _____
_____
_____
_____

I am good at: _____
_____
_____

I like to: _____
_____
_____

I do not like to:
_____
_____

I love to eat: _____
_____
_____
_____

My favorite book is: _____
_____
_____

My favorite subject is: _____
_____
_____

My favorite movie is: _____
_____
_____
_____

This is me!

My favorite animal is: _____
_____
_____

When I grow up, I want to be: _____
_____
_____
_____

Reprinted from TCM 457 Favorite Authors: Beverly Cleary, *Teacher Created Materials, 1994*

At-risk learners are especially aware of their level of ability and are constantly attempting to protect themselves from humiliation and embarrassment. During a literacy activity they may not try very hard, because if they do and become frustrated, they feel that it will make them look stupid. They already are quite self-conscious about their learning ability (or lack thereof), so they will tend to play it safe rather than take risks. Then, they fall behind the other students and are trying to catch up, which can become even more frustrating for them.

Regulating oneself is an ability that is acquired when gaining independence as a learner. To be self-regulated, a student draws on internalized strategies and competencies to complete tasks on his or her own. Students must learn to regulate themselves to achieve meaningful goals. This self-regulation ability greatly contributes to increased intentions to learn. At-risk learners take longer to develop self-regulation since their internal strategies may not be fully developed or used as frequently. Many at-risk students use the same strategies for different activities and cannot understand why they do not work well. For example, if a chapter in a book is assigned to be read in social studies class and some math problems are also assigned, different learning strategies will be used to complete the two different assignments. For the social studies assignment, the learner should use pre-reading, vocabulary, word analysis, and reading comprehension strategies; and for the math assignment, the learner should use computational strategies. Another difference between these two assignments is that the social studies assignment is more or less an individual one; whereas, the math assignment can be completed with the help of another (perhaps a parent, sibling, or a classmate). Discussing the problems and working them out through talking may help make the assignment a little easier. However, at-risk students tend to use the same learning strategies to accomplish both goals and may be afraid to ask for help. Knowing which strategies to use for varying tasks is a skill that is developed as the learner is challenged.

Having control over the tasks to be completed and being self-regulated constitutes self-determination. This is another key element we need to pay attention to. For teachers, the principle of ownership is a top priority and can be addressed during instructional scaffolding. Teachers who use instructional scaffolding encourage students to take control of the math, reading, writing, science, or social studies tasks to meet their own purposes and satisfy their own interests. Giving students the opportunities to take control of their own learning during the literacy event promotes ownership, an essential element in the development of motivation, positive attitudes towards

At-risk learners are especially aware of their level of ability and are constantly attempting to protect themselves from humiliation and embarrassment.

learning, and self-confidence.

Values and Beliefs

Family values and beliefs also play a major role in a learner's motivation, attitude, achievement, and self-confidence. These values and beliefs are rooted in families and communities, and they usually reflect the sociocultural differences among families. They may also reflect the differences between the home environment and the school environment. It is important for teachers to know how different cultures value literacy and learning. In all cultures learning is highly valued; the differences appear in the processes of learning and what information should be learned.

Some cultures use oral literacies more than written literacies. For example, storytelling is a significant part of the Native American and Hawaiian cultures. Passing stories from generation to generation is a long tradition that is continued today. It is important to know the different family values and beliefs your students bring to the classroom since they are influenced by these values and beliefs. However, sometimes what is valued in the home is not valued in the school environment. Clearly, there are sociocultural differences between the home culture and the school culture concerning the varied uses of literacy.

Sometimes, the expectations among students, parents, and teachers can contribute to a communication breakdown which interferes with learning. The communication lines must always be open in order for the most learning to occur.

In school, some students may experience a clash between their own values from home and the values of the school, including the proper language to speak. In school, Standard English is spoken and written; however, many children are not exposed to this until they enter school. In many homes, another language or dialect may be spoken, perhaps Spanish, Chinese, Russian, or Black English Vernacular (BEV). In these instances, the students almost need to learn a new language in school in addition to learning new subject matter.

It is important for you to know the values and beliefs of your students so that you show respect for everyone's values and beliefs. A wonderful, nonthreatening way to do this is to use the sample values activity on the following page. You may go over this with them individually at some point or just collect them and keep them for your own reference when designing lessons.

> Family values and beliefs also play a major role in a learner's motivation, attitude, achievement, and self-confidence.

Values

Name or Group Name _____

Everyone has a set of values by which he or she lives. Values are those beliefs or behaviors that are most important to an individual.

Complete the chart below, checking off the appropriate place on the value scale that matches your feelings about the item. There are no right or wrong answers. Just be true to yourself.

(1=valued, 2=somewhat valued, 3=not valued)

Item	Value Scale		
	1	2	3
Being liked			
Getting good grades			
Completing jobs or projects			
Having my parents' approval			
Being liked by my teacher			
Being funny			
Doing my best work			
Looking good			
Being neat			
Being honest			
Being appreciated			

Reprinted from TCM 654 Cooperative Learning Activities for Social Studies, *Teacher Created Materials, 1995*

Views of Literacy in School and at Home

Another clash between home and school environments may include the view of literacy that is important or the instructional routines that need to be followed, such as taking turns and sustained silent reading. This may result in low performances in literacy activities and achievement. An example of this is American Indian children, who are hesitant to talk in class because their culturally-shaped language use, acceptable in the home environment, is much different from that expected in school. The children perceive participation as requiring individual performance under the control of the classroom teacher. This can be quite confusing and frustrating for many students, especially for those who are at risk. This conflict can interfere with the learning that is expected of them in the classroom and create anxiety and fear. Their confusion may compel them to stay quiet, which can be misunderstood as being uninterested or not motivated.

The literacy activities in the home environment will vary according to socioeconomic status and cultural backgrounds, thus developing diverse values and beliefs. We know that literacy practices are present in all families, and we must acknowledge these practices and view school as an extension of these literacy practices or vice versa, view home as an extension of the school. Either way, we need to make the connection clear to the students to alleviate any pressure about separating their two worlds.

One example of making this connection is exemplified in a Hawaiian community in Honolulu. As a way to bridge the gap between the school and community, talk stories are used, a popular Hawaiian language pattern useful as a component of reading instruction (Au, 1980). The talk story pattern asks a question and encourages a few students to participate jointly in forming an answer. Through this activity, the students interact and respond to each other's answers, thus forming a group answer. This activity contrasts with the traditional classroom teacher-dominated recitation pattern, but it also shows a way to create compatibility between a school activity and a popular Hawaiian tradition. In this example, the teachers were able to utilize the knowledge of the family values and beliefs their students possessed and incorporated it into their lessons.

The family literacy practices that are used in the home and community greatly influence a learner. For many at-risk learners, however, there are few literacy practices that occur in their homes and communities, and often these kinds of practices are incongruent with those in the school environment. But there are ways to make them congruent, as was evidenced in the talk stories activity used in Hawaii. Similar ideas will be discussed in a later chapter.

> The family literacy practices that are used in the home and community greatly influence a learner.

In sum, purpose, goals, self-worth, self-regulation, self-determination, and family values and beliefs are all personal factors that can vary but will always influence a learner's intention to learn to some degree. Additionally, it is essential to remember that as previously stated, each learner will bring his/her inner thoughts, feelings, and beliefs to the literacy event, thus making it a personal process. So, it is important for teachers to expect various outcomes for activities and tasks. Each learner will bring something different to the task and will also take something different away. One activity can elicit many different learning outcomes, which is what makes for a diverse, exciting learning environment. In the next section, we will see how all of these personal factors can be influenced by the affective domain in the reader's head.

Factors Which Affect the Learning Outcome

The other personal factors that influence a learner in many different ways are called affective influences, those influences which affect the learning outcome. These consist of motivation, attitude, stance, response, and responsibility and can sway a learner one way or the other. Each one of these will be explained and discussed in detail, since they all influence a learner's engagement in literacy tasks across the curriculum. The affective influences are extremely important in the learning process, and they are usually overlooked or ignored. Fortunately, Ruddell and Unrau (1994) place high value on affective influences by stating, "affective conditions directly influence the reader's decision to read" (p. 1002). Therefore, these affective conditions also influence a writer's decision to write and an artist's decision to paint. This decision can shape the learner's intention, goals, and beliefs, for without these factors, the learning process is not complete.

Motivation is an affective factor which is extremely important to develop in at-risk learners. It is closely tied to attitude, another important affective factor. One's motivation, or desire to do something, is connected to the attitude towards that task or the subject matter. Since motivation is a difficult concept to define, it is easier to measure it according to the motivational drive, which can be high or low, or even fluctuate throughout the activity.

Sometimes a student may be motivated to do something, and as he/she progresses through the activity, the motivational drive may increase or decrease, based on the success the student achieves. This concept is quite similar for both young students and adults; the motivation level depends on the degree of success. Therefore, it is important for teachers to design variations of regular activities and lessons that will ensure success for those students who are at risk, while also

The other personal factors that influence a learner in many different ways are called affective influences, those influences which affect the learning outcome.

challenging them. If the activity begins as easy and then progressively gets difficult, a student is more likely to try it. On the other hand, if an activity begins as difficult, an at-risk student will avoid it altogether. You must set up the student for success and not failure. These students need as much reassurance and encouragement as they can possibly get; if they need to repeat some activities and feel successful over and over again, allow them to do so. This will build up their self-esteem and motivate them to try something slightly more difficult or the next activity in a sequence or unit.

Attitude Towards Learning

Attitude is so closely related to motivation and intention, it is hard to separate them; however, attitude certainly has its own place in the learning process. Attitude is a combination of the sociocultural view of values, beliefs, feelings, and prior experiences. One may define attitude as a positive or negative position, indicating a feeling or mood toward a person, group, object, situation, or value. This feeling is a combination of cognitive and affective emotions which express an opinion or a belief. This opinion or belief can influence the learner's purpose or the goal of the activity, as well as the attitudes of others. Purposes and incentives can also influence the learner as much as the belief that completing the task will bring pleasure or good grades, which relates to the internal motivations discussed in Chapter 1. Both of these factors (internal and external) will motivate the learner, thus contributing to the formation of attitude. It works in a cyclical fashion; attitude influences motivation, and motivation then influences attitude. It is a never-ending cycle, especially for at-risk learners.

> Attitude is a combination of the sociocultural view of values, beliefs, feelings, and prior experiences.

One important factor which can determine a person's attitude and promotes motivation is prior experiences with literature or content-area reading. Many students are either internally motivated to read or decide not to read based on past experiences related to reading. Having positive experiences, at home or in school, empowers learners with the self-confidence that they can read, write, compute, or draw by themselves or with another person, thus forming a positive attitude. Negative experiences may push a learner away from the whole idea of reading, writing, computing, or drawing, thus developing and maintaining a negative attitude. A learner remembers these experiences and activates these memories when confronted with reading instruction and pleasure reading in the classroom. If a learner is forced to read, he/she may turn away from it, just as when he/she is forced to do anything against his/her will, a negative attitude or feeling will develop. Development of a positive attitude toward learning is a key element in the learning process and can be developed in every classroom.

You can create motivation and positive attitudes within your classroom by providing many nongraded activities that allow the students to explore and discover without the fear of failure or the pressure to succeed. Also, giving more time to follow through on these activities motivates a student much more than giving a strict time limit which only adds pressure and self-doubt. At-risk learners may take a little longer to accomplish their goals, which means that they should have an equal chance to do just that. Once a student is motivated and feels confident, his/her attitude will change.

Sometimes a student may generalize his/her negative attitude toward the subject matter when, in fact, it is just a particular task he/she does not like to do. For example, if a student enjoys conducting science experiments and mixing chemicals but does not like writing up the observations and results, he/she may say he/she has a negative attitude toward science and will be less motivated to do that kind of work when, really, the learner has a negative attitude toward only a small task included within the subject matter. This confusion can cause a student to shy away from science-related activities and lose motivation to engage in these activities. If a student is aware that he/she could, perhaps, work with someone who does enjoy writing up the observations and results, his/her attitude may change and become more positive, and the motivation level may increase. Basically, it is important to let students know that attitude is not an all or nothing deal, and it is okay to change their attitudes with time.

> Like motivation, attitude is also a difficult term to define since many different perspectives can be taken.

Like motivation, attitude is also a difficult term to define since many different perspectives can be taken. Most of the definitions of attitude emphasize either evaluation, action, or feeling. There is a high correlation among the three aspects within a single attitude. Thus, the formation of an attitude depends upon many components, which makes it even more difficult to define but does not lessen its importance in the learning process, especially for students at risk. More likely, they will have negative attitudes towards learning based on prior negative experiences, but this can be changed by using your keen insight and support. Remember to take into consideration the students' attitudes when trying to motivate them to engage in a literacy task. You want to help them develop positive attitudes while motivating them to succeed.

Taking a Stance

A third affective factor which can heavily influence a learner is the stance, which is the perspective the learner will take toward a task. The stance helps a learner to focus his/her attention and purpose which in turn influences motivation, attitude, and intention. This is an opportunity for the learner to take control of the task and decide how to direct his/her attention. Although this is an internal factor in the learner's mind, it can be influenced by such external factors as the teacher and the classroom learning environment.

There is a belief that when reading, students experience texts through two stances: efferent and aesthetic. In efferent reading, the reader focuses on ideas and concepts to be taken away from the text; in aesthetic reading, the reader becomes absorbed in a text world of imagination and feelings in which the attention is focused on what the reader is living through during the reading event (Rosenblatt, 1978). The efferent stance is the popular stance used in many classrooms, which is much more regimented and prescriptive. The aesthetic stance allows the learner to explore the ideas in a more creative way. For example, an art project may be considered to be an activity in which the learner would choose the aesthetic stance to appreciate the beauty in the process and product. Science, on the other hand, tends to have more activities in which the learner would choose the efferent stance. The students are experimenting to find out specific information; therefore, they focus more on the general concepts to be taken away from the activity. For instance, if the project is to build a volcano and make it erupt, the typical stance the learner would choose is the efferent stance to learn the concept of volcanic eruptions. The aesthetic stance can also be chosen if part of the assignment is to make it look authentic, but otherwise, the efferent stance would more likely be chosen.

Social studies is a perfect example of a subject matter that can have activities that encourage students to take either one of the stances or both of them. Even if the assignment requires learning general concepts and ideas or specific names and dates, many activities can lend themselves to having the learner live through the experience. For instance, during a unit on the Civil War, students can read stories about it to learn some of the general understandings, such as why there was a war. What were they fighting over? What were the short-term and long-term effects of the war? Who fought in it? Where were the battles? In these activities, they would more likely choose the efferent stance in order to read to find out the answers. In another activity, such as coloring a map of the United States to show which states were in the Union, which states were in the Confederacy, and which ones were neutral, the students may choose the aesthetic stance, since coloring can be a creative task. While the students are coloring, they could pick a state and imagine what it would have been like to be a child living in that particular state during the war. These kinds of activities encourage students to take a stance toward the activity and realize that the stance can shift during the activity and that sometimes both stances can be taken.

> The aesthetic stance allows the learner to explore the ideas in a more creative way.

Stance affects the students' motivation by giving them the choice of which stance they want to adopt during the activity so they do not feel that there is only one way.

An Author's Stance

These same stances can be utilized in the area of writing. The author chooses a stance before writing, which helps decide the direction and tone of the piece. If the author wants to write an informative piece, he/she will choose the efferent stance; on the other hand, if the author wants to write a creative descriptive piece, the writer will choose the aesthetic stance, or sometimes the author will adopt both stances. For instance, if a student were to write a letter to another child living through the war, explaining what was going on in his/her town, the writer may choose the efferent stance at first, since he/she is inform-ing the other person; and, at the same time, the aesthetic stance can be taken so the writer can be very descriptive and creative.

> The author chooses a stance before writing, which helps decide the direction and tone of the piece.

It is important for students to know the different kinds of stances they can choose so they feel as though they have some choice in the task and some control over the outcome. Then, they will be more moti-vated and have a positive attitude towards the task. Also, so they do not approach every activity with the same attitude and feel they must use the same strategies to complete the task, it is helpful to the stu-dents if the teacher explains the assignment and reminds them that there is more than one way to accomplish the goal of the task. This is a worthy motivating strategy to use in your classrooms.

To further understand the importance of stance, it is essential to know that the learner selects a stance before the reading event, writ-ing event, math problem, social studies activity, or art project, according to the pre-determined purpose and goal. However, the stance can change at any point throughout the activity. It may be helpful to think of stance as a continuum, with one side being pre-dominantly efferent and the other side being predominantly aesthet-ic. Each literacy activity falls somewhere in the continuum, and most learners fluctuate between an efferent and an aesthetic stance.

An example of the activities that would fall on the continuum is shown below:

Predominantly◄----- Moderate -----► Predominantly efferent aesthetic		
A science chapter on planets for a test	The U.S.Constitution in social studies class	*The Cat in the Hat* for readers' theater

Reading a chapter on planets in a science text book for a test implies that the student will read to strictly gain information to study for the test. In social studies class, when reading the U.S. Constitution the student is reading to learn information but also can step into the text and relate to one of the authors of the document and imagine how this document has changed lives throughout history. When reading *The Cat in the Hat* for readers' theater, students are reading for the enjoyment and step into the story to read the text with imagination, emotion, and feeling.

During the reading event, a transaction between the reader and the text occurs. This text is not limited to a textbook but it can also be a piece of literature, a book, a magazine, a poem, a chapter in a science textbook, or any other content-area reading. Each time a learner begins to read, write, compute, draw, or experiment, it is a new and different experience. New transactions occur, and new outcomes arise. This transaction is the result of the learner stepping into the text, taking on the persona of the characters, and constructing meaning from the print on the page. The reader actively engages in the reading process and exerts control over the outcome, which is extremely important for at-risk learners. This issue of control or choice is a top priority for all learners, especially those at risk. As long as they feel they have some control of the activity, they will be more motivated to participate. By allowing them to choose their own stances, you are indirectly building their self-confidence, which is crucial for at-risk learners.

> **During the reading event, a transaction between the reader and the text occurs.**

In respect to reading literature or content-area reading, since each reader evokes different meanings from different texts through transaction, there can be a variety of interpretations, as well as a variety of understandings. Moreover, despite the differences in interpretations, each student is striving for a high level of comprehension and understanding. This belief allows readers to enjoy reading and create their own meanings, as opposed to trying to match the teacher's interpretation, falsely assuming the teacher's interpretation is the only correct understanding of the text. All readers must be allowed to enrich their linguistic abilities and personal experiences and freely draw upon them. The students must find a purpose in reading or take a stance towards the text, which will enable them to independently gain knowledge from new material.

Making Efferent Activities More Aesthetic
Some activities are naturally efferent or naturally aesthetic, and some can be both (when they fluctuate on the continuum). The challenge lies in making the efferent activities more aesthetic by allowing the students to enjoy the activity while extracting information. For

example, math activities are predominantly efferent; there is usually one right answer and the student computes the problem strictly to find out the correct answer. Integrating math activities with other subjects, such as social studies and language arts can help the students experience the joy of computing. For instance, in a lesson on computing averages you could integrate sports heroes and the sports section of a newspaper into math class and assign the students to compute batting averages of different baseall players from different teams. In addition to figuring out batting averages, the students could study the state and cities of the different teams, locate them on maps and then read some biographies about the players. This activity can be done with any sports statistics, which encourages the students to add, subtract, multiply, and divide numbers and information that has meaning for them and are not just abstract numbers. They are learning how to average numbers in an interesting way.

Many efferent activities can become more aesthetic if the students are allowed to bring in their personal life experiences and stories and integrate them into abstract lessons. For instance, while studying grammar, students can write letters to friends or relatives and exchange with partners to proofread for grammatical errors. Or, you can write a class letter on the overhead projector to a favorite author and teach about commas, colons, and letter formats. Although grammar may be an efferent activity at first, it is easy to make it more aethetic, which heightens your students' interest and motivation.

Some activities are naturally efferent or naturally aesthetic and some can be both (when they fluctuate on the continuum).

A Learner's Response to Activities and Tasks

An essential element in the learning process is that of response. It is important for students and teachers to discuss and talk about stories, activities, or experiments afterwards. This is a chance to reflect on the lesson and assess the outcomes. The best way to do this is to talk with your students and find out their reactions and observations. If we are encouraging students to transact with the text, step into the story, and write from the heart, we must also provide a forum for them to discuss their experiences. We know that we learn from each other, and this does not happen in silence or through mental telepathy; therefore, we need to plan time after activities and tasks for the learners to respond. This response can be oral or written, private or public. Learners' responses or reactions are closely connected to their motivations and attitudes toward learning, as well as the stances that are chosen for a subsequent activity.

A learner's response is somewhat affected by prior knowledge and experience. It is very important to remember that the learner brings to any activity personal goals, prior experiences, and excitement or fear.

Throughout the activity, the learner is evoking meaning and reacting to it; therefore, these feelings and emotions greatly influence the learner's stance and response. Afterwards, reflection on the meaning of the activity and the various interpretations and outcomes can be shared with one another. Therefore, when students are given time to respond and react to an activity, they are actively negotiating and constructing their own meanings, the ultimate goal in the learning process.

Commonly with aesthetic responses, the reader is able to transact with the text while creating visual images of the characters and setting. This idea closely connects to creating images and using background knowledge, which will be discussed in Chapter 3. Relating associations and feelings evoked, hypothesizing, extending, and retrospection are all included in the transaction with a text and response to the text. Response is a process of discovering meaning through talking and writing, which enables students to share ideas and negotiate new meanings. When students have the opportunity to talk or write about their own interests and ideas in response to the story, they develop a sense of ownership and voice, which leads to empowerment and responsibility.

A learner's response is somewhat affected by prior knowledge and experience.

For example, after reading *Strega Nona*, young students can discuss the old folk tale and their feelings about Big Anthony's problem when he does not listen. They can talk about the importance of listening and share their personal stories of when they did not listen to someone. After the discussion of the story, the students can make stick puppets and retell the story or make up their own stories with the same characters in the puppet theater using the example on the next page. Either way, the students are responding to the story and sharing ideas and feelings about the characters. In other words, they are transacting with the text and developing a sense of ownership and voice.

Stick Puppet Theaters

Make a class set of puppet theaters (one for each child) or make one theater for every 2–4 children. Stick puppet patterns and directions for making stick puppets are provided on pages 20–22.

Materials:

- 22" x 28" (56 cm x 71 cm) pieces of colored poster board (enough for each student or group of students)
- markers, crayons, or paints
- scissors or craft knives

Directions:

1. Fold the poster board 8" (20 cm) in from each of the shorter sides. (See picture below.)
2. Cut a window in the front panel, large enough to accommodate two or three stick puppets.
3. Let the children personalize and decorate their own theaters.
4. Laminate the stick puppet theaters to make them more durable. You may wish to send the theaters home at the end of the year or save them to use year after year.

Reprinted from TCM 436 Strega Nona Literature Unit, *Teacher Created Materials, 1993*

The Connection Between Stance and Response

Stance influences the goal and purpose of the literacy event as well as the focus for the task, which influences the learner's response and feelings toward the text. A response will differ if the reader is assigned to read to strictly gain information for a test rather than to read to enjoy the story and transact with the characters. Therefore, the response will range from pure delight to possible dislike or boredom.

The learner's stance and the learner's response are heavily influenced by the external factors of the teacher's instructional stance and the teacher's expectations. Poetry is a good example; often the teacher will expect the student to take the efferent stance and analyze each line of the poem instead of reading the entire poem for the aesthetic beauty. Additionally, stance can be influenced by parental expectations or family values and beliefs which become affective influences on a learner.

> **It is important for students to have the opportunity to respond to various literacy activities and stories written by classmates.**

During response time to literature, many students prefer the aesthetic stance because they like to discuss the images they have created during the story; also, they can discuss feelings that were evoked and some hypotheses they predicted. During this kind of discussion, there are no right or wrong answers, and the students feel at liberty to respond in their own ways. Additionally, this is a time for students to reflect on the story and negotiate meanings and ideas which can lead to higher levels of comprehension. For at-risk learners, this kind of response activity is very valuable to them, because they do not feel the pressure of guessing the right answer and can learn more about taking a stance toward the activity. Therefore, encouraging students to be creative and choose their own stances towards the text may help students develop higher level comprehension skills (e.g., analytical, applicative, and transactive). This is a goal for teachers when planning lessons and activities, to lead students to higher levels of comprehension and enjoyment. Allowing students to choose their own stances can be a critical step in accomplishing this goal.

It is important for students to have the opportunity to respond to various literacy activities and stories written by classmates. For at-risk learners, discussions are quite helpful. First of all, any questions can be discussed, which clears up some confusion. Secondly, some students are more expressive orally as opposed to writing, and they prefer to talk about the activity rather than becoming frustrated by trying to write down their responses. Additionally, the level of comprehension improves after a discussion. This discussion can be in a small group or the whole class, a chance for students to have their voices heard. This is assuming the atmosphere of the classroom learning environment is a safe one where all learners feel comfortable speaking their opinions.

Responsibility for Learning

There are many internal factors that influence and promote the desire for, and the enjoyment of, learning. It does not matter how many external factors are present, because ultimately it is an internal motivation that is the driving force. One of these internal forces that can be motivational is the responsibility that learners assume for their own learning. This internal motivation empowers an individual to make the decision to learn something and to develop an attitude towards learning. These internal factors can be a combination of cultural or family values and beliefs, self-perceived goals, purposes, time elements, and the desire or intention. If the learner has the "want to" and enough time to enjoy the activity or task in a comfortable social context, he/she will take on the responsibility for learning.

Teachers can increase internal motivation by allowing students to make decisions about their learning and providing time for the learning to occur. Internal motivations develop over time and through various experiences.

Teachers can increase internal motivation by allowing students to make decisions about their learning and providing time for the learning to occur.

This idea of the learner's responsibility relates to Covington's connection between motivation and self-worth, which was previously discussed in Chapter 1. It is believed that self-worth, as perceived by the student, strongly affects the degree to which the student becomes an effective learner in the instructional setting (the classroom). This self-worth helps the learner take on responsibility for his/her own learning and develop an attitude about him/herself. The level of confidence, a feeling of competence, and a sense of control are all tied to self-worth and, ultimately, to his/her learning capacity and achievement. If a student feels control over the desired outcome, he/she will take responsibility for a successful performance. If students feel they have little control over the outcome, they will not take responsibility for a failed performance. This is a sensitive subject, especially for at-risk learners who have experienced frustration and failure in the past.

Concluding Remarks

In conclusion, it is evident how these affective influences play a prominent role in the learning process. These factors, motivation, attitude, stance, response, and responsibility, can heavily sway a learner's intention to learn and to continue learning. All of these factors are personal; that is, they will vary from learner to learner. Therefore, teachers must be aware of these different factors and be prepared to deal with them in the classroom learning environment. These factors strongly influence a learner to engage in a literacy task and choose to stay with and complete the task. For many at-risk learners, these affective factors have the most influence on them. If they do not have a positive attitude toward the subject matter, they will not have the motivation to engage in activities and tasks in that particular subject. As the classroom teacher, one of your goals is for all students to be motivated to engage in literacy tasks across the curriculum and develop a positive attitude towards learning. Knowing about the personal factors your students bring with them into the classroom can help you help them.

Cognitive Factors Influencing Learners

Inside the Learner's Head

Now that you have become familiar with the personal and affective factors that influence the learner, I will discuss the influences within the learner's head, which are called cognitive influences. They require thinking skills, as opposed to the affective influences which rely more heavily on feelings and emotions. These cognitive influences definitely play a prominent role in the learning process, specifically in background knowledge and schema, creating images (or imagery), self-monitoring skills, and word analysis skills. This chapter will define each of these influences and explain the interconnectedness of them. These influences constantly interact with the affective influences described in the previous chapter to help a learner learn and comprehend the subject matter.

> Background knowledge is the learner's knowledge base for literacy development.

Background Knowledge and Schema

Background knowledge is the learner's knowledge base for literacy development. It is the knowledge one gains throughout a lifetime and stores in the memory or what cognitive psychologists call schema. The information is stored in schemata which are like little containers into which we deposit our particular experiences that we have and the knowledge that we gain. When we learn something new, we tap into our schema, which is a structure that facilitates retrieval of information from memory and contributes to the reconstruction of new knowledge, thus playing a crucial role in the comprehension process. Theories about schema, and the importance of background knowledge, broke through in the 1970s and caused a great deal of excitement for theoreticians, researchers, and, most importantly, practitioners. Schema theory was a momentous breakthrough because it encouraged teachers to be positive and to ask, "What does this learner already know about this particular subject?" and "How can I use that to help him/her deal with these new ideas?" rather than the negative perspective of "What is it that this learner does not know?" and "How can I get this information into his/her head?" This was, and still is, a significant advance in working with at-risk students. It is extremely important to be positive, to give them confidence, and to build on what they do know.

> In recent years, there has been an emphasis on the importance of background knowledge in the learning process.

In recent years, there has been an emphasis on the importance of background knowledge in the learning process. As discussed earlier, a learner's intention, stance, and response are influenced by the learner's background knowledge and experiences. Also included in a learner's background knowledge, which leads to better comprehension, is the ability to evoke prior declarative, procedural, and conditional knowledge. The declarative knowledge is thought of as the "what" strategies needed for understanding the subject matter text (which is not exclusive to books, but can also refer to a conversation, a science experiment, or an event in history). The procedural knowledge includes the plans or strategies that the learner will use during the problem-solving process. Some of these "how" strategies may include decoding, use of context clues, and skimming for reading. For science, they may include observing, investigating, hypothesizing, and recording results. Finally, the conditional knowledge helps the learner decide when to use which procedural strategies and why their application is useful in the learning process. These processing strategies help a learner understand not only the what of the text but also understand the how, the when, and the why. It may be helpful to explain to your students that there are different strategies to be used and to teach them how and when to use them.

These three kinds of knowledge, declarative, procedural, and conditional, are acquired as learners progress from novices to experts and are stored in the those little containers in our memory. These knowledge structures have slots that are filled with specific information learned from past experiences. For instance, if we see a car, we store that visual experience into our car schema. If we go to an ice cream shop, we store that experience in our ice cream schema. If we go to the movies, we store that in our movie schema, etc. Every learner possesses a different schema structure which is unique to that individual. The information is stored in one schema and links are made between schemas that are associated with each other.

At-risk students do not automatically tap into their background knowledge and experiences and make associations between background knowledge and new knowledge when reading or writing. Also, they may use their declarative and procedural knowledge but are not sure when to use these particular strategies; therefore, they tend to use the same strategies for every task, which can cause frustration. Sometimes these students are even unable to find the correct slot within the particular schemata, and then the text does not make any sense to them. More often than not, they do not have enough background knowledge to understand a new experience or text, which can also create a frustrating situation.

Every learner possesses a different schema structure which is unique to that individual.

The interesting aspect of schema theory is that everyone has his/her own schemata. Therefore, it will vary from individual to individual, depending on the reader's culture, prior knowledge and experiences. For example, if a student is reading E.B. White's (1952) story *Charlotte's Web*, the background knowledge of the student will greatly influence the level of comprehension. If the student lives in an urban environment, he/she may not have much experience or information about a farm or farm life. However, if the student lives in a rural environment, he/she will likely have more background information about a farm and how to take care of animals and thus, attain a higher level of comprehension about the story.

As the reader is reading, he/she is synthesizing the material and activating schema. When a reader activates schemata while transacting with the text, he/she is also predicting what will happen next, based on the knowledge he/she already has. A writer also experiences this activation of schema when writing a story and trying to figure out what will happen next or how to end the story. Actually, in all learning situations we tap into our schema to find out if we have any previous knowledge stored in our memories that can help us learn new material. We do this subconsciously and are not aware of how we retrieve the information or how we make the associations; it just naturally happens. However, for at-risk learners, this process is not natural; therefore, it can be difficult and frustrating.

Creating Images While Learning
In addition to schema theory, imagery is another form of mental processing that occurs when a child reads, writes, computes, or draws.

Creating images to represent words is not a new concept. Thousands of years ago, Plato used a wax tablet to express his thoughts through pictures and images. Many children do this as emergent readers and writers by drawing pictures and continue to do so mentally as they become skilled learners. In the learning process, both the language (in the verbal system) and the mental imagery (in the nonverbal system) are important to achieve comprehension.

Nonverbal images, in fact, play a vital role in the learning process, especially when students have the opportunity to talk about the text. For example, in a reading group when readers respond to the text, they share the visual images they create in their minds while reading. They also respond to the images in addition to responding to the dialogue or plot of the story. These images assist others in responding as well, which makes imagery a necessary element in the learning process and strengthens the connection between the cognitive and affective influences on the learner.

> Most learners enjoy creating images in their minds as they read, write, compute, measure, and experiment.

Most learners enjoy creating images in their minds as they read, write, compute, measure, and experiment. In some subject areas, such as science and social studies, many images are provided for the learner to make the association between the text language and the visual images. For instance, in a social studies unit about Westward Expansion in the 1800s, a third grader may find a book that has many pictures of the covered wagons, trail maps, and some heroes and heroines of the Wild West, including Bill Pickett and Annie Oakley. Although some images may be provided, the learner can be motivated to create his/her own images of the journey of the settlers. Together, language and images aid in comprehension of the material.

As an example, while students are designing a map key and naming trails, they can create images of what it was like to travel from St. Louis to Kansas City. Also, as a math activity, students can use the distance scale from a reference book to determine the length of each trail. During this activity they will create images in their minds and share them with classmates or keep the images to themselves; either way, they are creating images while learning. Imagery is an essential element in the learning process, especially for at-risk learners. They should be encouraged to create images and talk about the ones they conjure up in their own minds. Learners have very different images of the same story or subject matter, and if they have a chance to share these images and interpretations, they will learn more.

Self-Monitoring

The self-monitoring and self-correcting strategies a learner uses during the learning process are known as metacognition, or rather, thinking about thinking. Self-monitoring is not only the awareness of one's own cognitive processes but also the deliberate directions of one's own efforts and selection of strategies. Additionally, self-monitoring is the skill that a learner develops by experimenting with various strategies to see which ones work for which particular activities. Knowing when to stop and change strategies is also part of self-monitoring.

In order to understand more clearly how all of this works, we must remember an important aspect of learning is understanding how to use strategies to assist comprehension and that specific knowledge and motivation are critical to becoming a strategic learner. The ultimate goal for every learner is to become a strategic one, to know what strategies to use and when to use them. This relates to the declarative, procedural, and conditional knowledge that learners gain as they progress from novice to intermediate or expert learners. Unfortunately, many at-risk learners progress at a slower pace and never quite learn which strategies to use and when to use them.

> The ultimate goal for every learner is to become a strategic one, to know what strategies to use and when to use them.

This cognitive development happens in the social context of learners in the classroom through collaboration and group sharing. Being a strategic learner takes practice, and those who are skilled make the choices of how much time and effort will be expended on the particular task, thus increasing or decreasing motivation. However, at-risk learners are not able to make the same choices because they have difficulty keeping track of comprehension goals and strategies if decoding requires all of their attention. In the case of reading, time and attention are extremely important, and beginning readers, as well as less skilled readers, spend too much time on decoding and, therefore, have no time or energy left for comprehension or discussion. Usually, this is the case with at-risk learners or the reason why they struggle so much with reading and writing.

In strategy use, the motivation, attitude, and intention of the learner are extremely important, especially for those at risk. For example, if the student wants to read *Anne Frank: The Diary of a Young Girl* to find out more about living through a war and hiding from the Nazis, before the reading event, the reader decides on a strategy which takes time and effort. One strategy may be to brainstorm ideas about World War II and look at a world map to locate Amsterdam, Holland, the setting of the story. Another strategy may be to trade places with Anne or to trade places with her father and read the story with the perspective of that character. The reader needs to be interested in accomplishing the goal that was set forth at the beginning, and if the reader is interested in accomplishing this goal, then the time and effort will be exerted and the self-monitoring strategies will be used throughout the reading activity. Then, afterwards, responding to the texts contributes to the further development of self-monitoring skills. It provides the student time to think about what he/she has read and what he/she has learned. This time also provides the learner with a chance to reflect on the material and draw some conclusions on his/her own, as well as with the group.

Word Analysis Skills

Since reading is required in all content areas, we cannot ignore the importance of word analysis skills which provide information that enables the reader to transform the print into words and then into meaning. This knowledge base expands from preschool experiences, beginning with print and invented spelling, to the later grades where such skills are used in the analysis of new words and in automatic processing of previously known words. For beginning readers, word analysis is when they first encounter printed letters together on a page. What do readers do?

For beginning readers, word analysis is when they first encounter printed letters together on a page.

Instruction in word analysis must occur in a meaning-based context regardless of whether you are teaching from a phonics-based program or from a whole-language or literature-based program. Readers progress through developmental phases when acquiring word analysis knowledge. These four phases include logographic, which uses cues relying on visual contextual or graphic features to read words; transition from logographic to beginning alphabetic, which starts to connect the printed letters to sounds and pronunciation; alphabetic, which is characterized by the ability to use letter-sound relationships to read words; and, finally, orthographic, which uses alphabetic principles but also predictable letter patterns and groups in orthographic neighborhoods that form patterns larger than sound-letter correspondences (Ehri, 1991).

Your goal is to assist students in the development of these skills so they become automatic. Learners progress through these stages at different rates; many at-risk learners progress at a slower rate if they have had little or no experience with print and books. As the reader becomes more skilled in word analysis, he/she reaches a point when he/she automatically recognize a word without having to decode it. Once a learner reaches this point, more time can be devoted to comprehension as opposed to exerting all of his/her energy on decoding each word. Time is needed for this process to happen, and for at-risk readers additional time is needed for comprehension, since they tend to spend too much time on decoding.

Comprehension

Throughout the learning process, the learner's personal factors and affective and cognitive influences all contribute to the negotiation of meaning construction or comprehension of the subject matter. The meaning construction factor incorporates the comprehension strategies a reader uses throughout the scope of learning. Since reading and writing with comprehension is a goal of every learner, this component is an essential element in the learning process. Comprehension of text results from analyzing words, activating schema, and relating previous knowledge with new knowledge to construct meaning.

Many of the personal, affective, and cognitive factors are influential on comprehension. Additionally, the meaning construction factor is heavily influenced by external factors, such as the teacher's instructional strategies and the home environment, as well as the internal factors of prior knowledge and experience. Instruction is designed to help students build understandings for curricular goals. Experience is the fuel for schema development. It simply provides helpful information, which students build upon as they learn and understand different concepts and ideas. Additionally, children need to know that they can bring their experiences into the classroom and into their own comprehension process. Unfortunately, many children feel that what they do at home or outside of school is not related or relevant to what they are learning in school. Therefore, they do not activate their schema as much as possible and make those connections between prior knowledge and present experiences. This is an area that must be addressed by teachers in all content areas. Students should be encouraged to bring in home or community experiences and bridge the gap. If a student sees that all of his/her experiences can help him/her learn, he/she will feel confident and less afraid to use personal experiences as a springboard for learning.

Many of the personal, affective, and cognitive factors are influential on comprehension.

While your students are learning, they are intersecting or linking previous knowledge to new knowledge to construct and reconstruct meanings and increase comprehension. Learners are constantly using prior knowledge to gain information and construct meaning from new knowledge and experiences. This idea can be applied to the overall learning process. In all subject matters, students construct and reconstruct meanings and invariably use prior knowledge and experiences to learn. At-risk learners need to be encouraged to reconstruct meanings when new knowledge is learned. Many times, if they try to understand new information and are unsuccessful, they give up instead of trying again at a later time. This concept is unfamiliar to them; they do not realize that meaning can be constructed and reconstructed in their own thoughts rather than just one way.

Before, during, and after an activity, the students' knowledge bases are invariably expanding. The more they read, talk, write, draw, measure, experiment, imagine, and share, the more knowledge they will gain and the more their prior knowledge will grow, which, in turn, strengthens their ability to construct meaning. This knowledge is gained through all kinds of engaged literacy activities, independently, with partners, or in large groups. The more discussion that is provided, the more knowledge a student will add to his/her schemata for future literacy development. This knowledge is provided before the literacy activity, when the purpose, goal, and stance are determined, as well as after the reading event during the reader response discussions. Once again, the connecting links between personal factors and the cognitive and affective influences are strengthened, which intensely influence the level of comprehension.

Concluding Remarks

In summation, the cognitive influences weigh heavily on the learner's intention and desire to learn. It is important to remember that all of the personal, affective, and cognitive factors influence the at-risk learner. Additional external factors in the classroom also influence the learner and will be explained in the next chapter about the classroom learning environment. It must be emphasized that although many of these factors are discussed separately, they can overlap, interact, transact, and have direct, as well as indirect, influences on one another. They all contribute to the learning process in their own unique ways for each individual.

In summation, the cognitive influences weigh heavily on the learner's intention and desire to learn.

Creating a Positive
Learning Environment

Invitation to Learn

Imagine you are a third grader who has struggled with reading, has developed a negative attitude toward reading, and, therefore, lacks the motivation to read. Upon entering an elementary classroom, a child will look around and see evidence of literacy everywhere, words written on the blackboard, labels on the walls and closets, calendars, schedules, classroom rules, and, most importantly, lots of books, picture books, textbooks, and informational books. This entrance into such a learning environment can be daunting.

The process of learning is a challenge for every student, especially for at-risk learners, who have previously experienced frustration and failure. Therefore, it is extremely important for the learning environment to be warm and inviting to all students. There should be many opportunities to engage in various literacy activities that allow experimentation with reading, writing, speaking, listening, computing, drawing, and discovering. Group sharing and independent exploration of literacy is an essential part of a positive learning environment. Ultimately, every classroom should create interest in learn-

The process of learning is a challenge for every student, especially for at-risk learners, who have previously experienced frustration and failure.

39

ing, so much so that students feel motivated to read and write and participate in various activities.

Our classrooms need to motivate students to use literacy to reach beyond the classrooms, schools, and communities into all aspects of their lives. The teacher and the classroom learning environment play a vital role in the literacy development of at-risk learners by stimulating those internal motivations and creating the interest and desire to learn within the classroom. The external motivating factors within the classroom include the setting, engaged literacy activities, the element of time, the teacher's instructional strategies, and language interaction. Combined with additional factors, a positive learning environment can be created for all learners, especially those at risk.

Our classrooms need to motivate students to use literacy to reach beyond the classrooms, schools, and communities into all aspects of their lives.

All of these factors are integrated within the physical aspects of the room to create the classroom learning environment which provides the interest and motivation to learn. While these factors overlap, interrelate, and interact with one another, intention, desire, and interest are included in all of these areas and are the result of the combination of these various influences.

Historically, the importance of the physical environment in learning and literacy development has been emphasized by many theorists and philosophers. According to Piaget, children acquire knowledge by interacting with the world or the environment (Piaget & Inhelder, 1969). In the classroom learning environment, children can assimilate new experiences into what they already know. Learning takes place as the child interacts with peers and adults in social settings and conducive environments (Vygotsky, 1978). Based on these theories, the classroom should be designed to provide optimum literacy development through rich literacy activities across the curriculum that include reading, writing, speaking, listening, experimenting, computing, and drawing.

The Social Context

The setting, or social and physical surroundings, are important for many reasons, especially in a learner's intention and desire to learn. It must be compatible with the activity, or else the learner will not feel very comfortable. For instance, if a student is reading in the library corner and the rest of the class is singing a song with a record, the student who is trying to read will feel uncomfortable or will not be able to concentrate. On the other hand, if the classroom is dull and boring and a learner wants to talk about the results from a science experiment with his/her partners, the setting is not compatible with that activity and may deter the learner from initiating this important discussion.

Often, the setting is not compatible with the activity for the at-risk reader; there are too many distractions which interfere. Their attention span is usually shorter, and they are not very focused; however, if they are out of the busy classroom and working in a smaller, quieter room with only one activity going on, chances are they will fare much better. Unfortunately, this may be an idealistic situation.

External influences in the classroom, such as peer interaction and teacher interaction, often provide learners with a purpose and a goal for learning, which combine with the learning environment to influence the learner. The classroom environment should promote autonomy, which, in turn, will have a positive effect on the student's intrinsic motivation for learning. Thus, the social context is crucial in the development of internal motivations and positive attitudes towards learning, especially for at-risk learners.

The Internalization Process

Internalization is essential in the motivational process. It consists of a series of transformations; first, a student reconstructs an activity that initially was external, and then an interpersonal process is transformed into an intrapersonal one after a long series of developmental events.

For instance, when the teacher reads a book to a group of young children, he/she probably sits in the front of the group and holds the book up so all the children can see the pictures, and while reading the story he/she can point to the pictures. Later on, a student may pretend to be the teacher and sit in front of a friend or a sibling and read a story while holding up the book and pointing to the pictures. This is an example of an external activity (an interpersonal process) tranforming into an intrapersonal one. At first the student watches the activity and observes and then internalizes it and performs it on his/her own.

This notion of internalization of the activity of reading relates to Rosenblatt's (1978) theory of transaction in which the student is continually in transaction with the environment. Within the social context, there are many transactions with the environment, the peers, the teacher, and the text. At-risk learners need to understand that learning occurs through these different transactions, and not only between the learner and the text (or assignment).

The Importance of Social Interaction

Social learning occurs within the social context when the student's experience involves social activity in the sense that he or she participates in interactions involving one or more persons. The very

> The classroom environment should promote autonomy, which, in turn, will have a positive effect on the student's intrinsic motivation for learning.

41

processes or relationships that are involved in social interaction are eventually taken over and internalized by the child to form individual cognitive processes, a genetic law of cultural development (Vygotsky, 1978). Any function appears first between people and then within the child. Many at-risk learners may not internalize the social interactional patterns and processes, which then causes confusion.

The importance of the social activities happening in the classroom learning environment is tremendous. There is an inexhaustible amount of mental and physical activity in the classroom from which each child can gain different knowledge in every social interaction. Reading and language development are two of the most important social interaction activities happening within the classroom context. And these happen within writing activities, science experiments, math games, and social studies projects, as well as music performances and art activities. Sometimes even physical fitness activities require reading, writing, speaking, and listening, which indirectly develop language. For many at-risk students, non-academic activities are less threatening. Although a music or art activity may also include reading and/or writing, the learner does not feel that is the main focus of the activity and may feel more confident. Remember, the learner must feel a sense of competence and control with the activity before he/she decides to participate.

The importance of the social activities happening in the classroom learning environment is tremendous.

Providing Motivational Opportunities

A positive learning and reading environment also includes exposure to literature of all genres; this can be accomplished through a library corner or classroom bookstore. If the literature is visibly present and an integral part of the classroom, it is difficult for students to ignore it. The literature must be accessible to all students and not kept in a special area where only privileged students (or those who get their work done first) can go. If that is the case, the teacher makes it easy for at-risk learners to shy away and distance themselves.

Every classroom should provide motivational opportunities and many activities at various levels of difficulty that are challenging and also fun. Opportunities to transact with the text should also be included in many activities that span across the curriculum. Encouraging a learner to become a character by dressing up and acting out a favorite scene from a book is a great way for the learner to transact with the text. Frequently, at-risk learners would rather do an activity such as that instead of writing out a book report or answering questions about a story.

Peer interaction, as well as teacher-student interaction, is a consequential component of a classroom learning environment. Students learn so much from other students through structured activities such as reader response groups and free play. Teacher-student interaction is the essence of the learning environment and the learning process. These interactions should not be noisy and loud; rather, these interactions can occur in a quiet, small group discussion or during recess time.

Additional Elements to Consider

A challenging reading program for every student should be offered, and enough time to enjoy the learning process should also be included in the planning of lessons and designing of a learning environment. Through various literacy activities, the teacher can create interest and motivation in reading and writing for all students in all areas, especially those at risk.

Other factors within the social context that need to be mentioned are the various cultural backgrounds of students and peer pressure. The learner's cultural background affects expectations for literacy uses in the classroom and expectations for future use of literacy activities; because of this, the learner's use of the immediate environment may not focus on the importance of activities leading to literacy. As the child matures, the peer group becomes increasingly instrumental in determining the effectiveness of classroom interaction with the teacher and with the text. Peer pressure can influence a reader's intention to read positively and negatively.

Other factors within the social context that need to be mentioned are the various cultural backgrounds of students and peer pressure.

The Element of Time

A woven thread throughout this book is the element of time and how crucial this is for at-risk learners. We may not give much thought to it as we scramble through each day, and we are always amazed at how fast the time goes. Just think of how frustrated we feel when we cannot get through the wonderful lesson we planned for our class. This is how at-risk learners feel regularly. They feel hurried and frustrated. We need to be reminded of this as we plan lessons and set up our room for centers, stations, or other kinds of activities. Time is an essential and valuable element in the learning process, which needs to be written into all lessons. It is imperative to assure proper amounts of time for lessons and units, which means negotiating between content areas and integrating lessons across the curriculum. This could even be the key to success, especially for those at risk. If follow up activities and extension activities are offered, it gives the students more time to absorb new information and internalize it.

The following example of a science lesson will further illustrate the point that we must keep in mind the amount of time allotted to instruction, experimenting, observing, investigating, and responding, which has a great deal of influence on both the student's attitudes and motivation. For example, during a lesson on leaves in the plant unit, the students need time to classify the many types of leaves found in their area and brainstorm ideas about the differences among leaves. Then the instruction part of the lesson consists of introducing plant vocabulary and showing some examples of plant leaves. If the students do not have any leaves that they have brought in from home, they need time to take a nature walk to gather leaves. When they have some leaves, then they need time to examine them and label the parts of the leaves (i.e., apex, vein, base), and then they can compare with their friends. Findings can be compiled on a graph by each student or by the whole class. Afterward, students can respond to such questions as, "What is the most common margin?" "Can there be more than one margin on any one leaf?" "How can leaf margins help classify plants?" and so on. This whole lesson takes a good deal of time for the student to learn about leaves, examine them, and respond to questions about them. So, the teacher should teach the lesson over a few days or extend the lesson time by integrating other content areas.

Leaf Reference Sheet

Leaves . . .

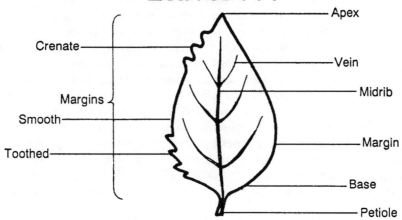

- Apex
- Vein
- Midrib
- Margin
- Base
- Petiole

- Crenate
- Margins
- Smooth
- Toothed

Types of Leaves

Compound   Simple

Leaf Attachments

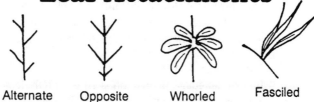

Alternate   Opposite   Whorled   Fasciled

Leaf Shapes

Lanceolate   Oblong   Ovate   Dissected   Elliptical   Oval   Linear

Reprinted from TCM 629 Plants Thematic Unit, *Teacher Created Materials, 1994*

However, merely allocating time for reading, writing, or responding is not nearly as important as what happens during that time. In a language arts lesson, if a child is given time to read for aesthetic purposes as well as for efferent purposes, the experience may be more rewarding. The more time a child has to read for enjoyment, the more motivated he/she may become, because the child will not always feel pressured to read fast just to find out the answers. Extra time and less pressure may result in improved reading achievement. If enough time is allotted, motivation and attitude may also increase, in addition to academic achievement. Time should be given for all reading, not only during reading class but in all classes. Reading across the curriculum should be emphasized; thus, the combination of allotted time segments from each content area adds up to a significant amount of time devoted to reading for different purposes. Even in math class, students need to read the directions or problems they are working on. They also need time to compare answers and discuss the process they went through to compute their answers.

> The ability to think is such a valuable tool, we must not take it for granted, and we must not waste it.

It is very important to remember that time should also be allotted for responding to texts, whether it is a oral discussion with the whole class, a silent discussion in the mind of the learner, or even a written response. So much of the value of the learning experience comes from thinking about, talking about, or writing about the work. While we are philosophically thinking about time for reader response, we must not forget the timeless words of John Dewey (1938), who said, "An activity—even the activity of reading—doesn't become an experience until we think about it" (p. 46). The ability to think is such a valuable tool, we must not take it for granted, and we must not waste it. When a learner is given time to negotiate and construct meaning from the text, he/she is able to store it into his/her memory to be activated at a later time. Also, the learner may develop positive feelings towards the subject matter if there are no time restrictions.

Language Interaction
Indeed, language interaction is an essential element in the learning and comprehension process (i.e., setting the purpose and goal, choosing a stance, responding to the text, and negotiating meaning). For at-risk learners, language development and interaction become especially important to be active participants in the literacy community of the classroom. In order for students to communicate with each other and the teacher, they first need to learn the language and feel comfortable enough to speak in the classroom. This can apply to both at-risk learners and second-language learners, and if they are one and the same, it is even more important to encourage language interaction. The key word, of course, is interaction, which means the classroom may get a little noisy. It is virtually impossible to maintain a

silent classroom and encourage language development at the same time.

Children are constantly trying to make sense of their worlds and obtain meaning, and this can happen only in a language rich environment which affords them opportunities to interact with peers and adults. This emphasizes the importance of the external factors in the classroom learning environment, which motivate the learner to respond, discuss, and negotiate new meanings and ideas.

Language is developed in social relations and interaction with others. Language development is also critical to a child's comprehension ability, which in the case of emergent readers and writers must be developed on an oral level before they begin to read or write for themselves. Participation in social dialogue is extremely important, and the child's emerging control of any symbol system is simultaneously the child's increasingly active participation in a cultural dialogue, for symbol systems contain a people's way of organizing and responding to experience (Dyson 1991). Through dialogue with others, children enter into "the social history of the imagination." (Dyson, 1991).

> **Language is developed in social relations and interaction with others.**

Interaction reveals the social desires, expectations, and even the resources of writers and readers, especially, in the classroom. Providing engaged literacy activities promotes language interaction and creates a forum for students to talk, discuss, negotiate, and respond, which are all parts of a language development program. "An oral language program should include many opportunities for students to use listening and speaking for genuine purposes" (Loban, 1963, p. 89). We should all take this advice as we think about setting up our classrooms and designing our lessons.

Concluding Remarks

As evidenced in the preceding discussion, together, the teacher and the classroom learning environment play extremely important roles in the literacy development and motivation of the learner. The social interaction that takes place during literacy instruction in the classroom and the time to enjoy it contributes to the literacy development of each student. The classroom is a very busy social arena where most of a child's learning takes place. Within this social context, there is a generous amount of language interaction between the teacher and students, meaningful literacy tasks for the students to engage in, and activities that provide opportunities for literacy growth and development. These opportunities should develop all areas of literacy and lead to motivations to learn math, science, social studies, and language arts.

Social interaction is an essential element in creating a positive learning environment, which is synonymous with building a classroom community. To become a member of the classroom community, a student needs to participate in the activities valued by the class, many of which require social interaction and dialogue, such as math games, reader's theater, and science experiments. The young students in your classrooms come from various backgrounds, speak many languages, and bring their diverse experiences to each activity. These varied backgrounds and experiences should be shared in class discussions and through social interactions, helping one another learn. Since interactions occur on a daily basis in the classroom community among students and between teachers and students, it is through these interactions that knowledge is transferred and students' knowledge is transformed. The social interaction between students and adults is an integral component in the learning process, and inevitably, both gain some valuable knowledge from the experience which can be useful in future literacy development. The interactions create experiences students use to learn new knowledge and build on prior knowledge, hence, all ideas and meanings are connected to interactions and experiences. Therefore learning to read, write, compute, draw, discover, and explore happens through social interactions and the dialogue with others in a positive learning environment.

Instructional Strategies and Assessment Practices

The Teacher's Role

The teacher plays a pivotal role in the learning process for every student. As adults, when we look back on our early educational careers, we often think of a teacher who was influential in one way or another. Perhaps it was because she was so nice, or he was funny, or she believed in you. When people ask why you became a teacher, it is because you were positively influenced early on and wanted to play an important role in another person's life. Whatever the reason may be, we have all heard our calling and find ourselves on center stage on a daily basis. Our students look to us for guidance, knowledge, reassurance, and some tender loving care. Our at-risk students look to us for motivation and inspiration, as well as encouragement and support. We can provide all of this and more in our classroom learning environment not only in the way we set up our classrooms but, more importantly, in the way we plan our lessons, using a variety of instructional strategies and assessment practices. It is always helpful to have an assortment of strategies to use for all different activities. The following suggestions are meant to add to your repertoire and to use at your own discretion. Also, these are valuable strategies to

> Our at-risk students look to us for motivation and inspiration, as well as encouragement and support.

49

share with parents of your at-risk learners. If the same strategies are used in school and at home, you are building that bridge that your students desperately want to cross, and you are breaking down barriers that may interfere with their learning. Go ahead and share these at parent-teacher conferences or Back-to-School Night. If you send home a parent newsletter, in each issue you could highlight one of your many instructional strategies and assessment practices. However you choose to disseminate this information, you help your students tremendously.

Teacher's actions should be designed to increase their students' motivation and interest in learning.

Teacher's actions should be designed to increase their students' motivation and interest in learning. Frequently, teachers provide engaging reading and writing activities in combination with other meaningful literacy tasks, such as math games, a science experiment, or a social studies reenactment. Also, teachers implicitly or explicitly provide the purpose and goal for the lesson and determine the stance a learner should take toward the text, either aesthetic or efferent. Remember the text can be a book, a magazine, a math problem, or a science lab experiment. It is quite apparent how the learner's stance is heavily influenced by the teacher's stance, which can fall in a continuum and is shifting throughout a lesson or across lessons. The teacher's stance also influences the activities provided for the students to engage in, which should vary from those with an aesthetic stance to those with an efferent stance. Additionally, the teacher's stance will influence the form of assessment used to evaluate the students.

Ultimately, teachers are creating a literacy community within the classroom; therefore, the instructional strategies and assessment practices that are used will contribute to the creation and development of the learners' motivations to learn within this literacy community. The teacher's belief in her/his students helps to create a positive learning environment. If the teacher believes that all children can learn, she/he will promote literacy development; however, if the teacher believes that at-risk learners lack the ability to learn, he/she may not promote literacy development as much for them. We want to avoid this situation. I know that all teachers believe that all of their students have ability and that even those who are at-risk can succeed in their classrooms.

Although the following strategies can be applied to all students, they are most helpful for your at-risk students since they provide many motivational opportunities for them to get involved in their own learning. These strategies can help them become active participants in the literacy community of the classroom.

The Beginning: Designing Appropriate Lessons

A teacher's instructional strategies include designing lessons that aim to foster a sense of competence, self-control, and purpose. If these elements are included, the learner's motivation and responsibility are activated; then, the activities will become naturally rewarding for the students. This strategy is especially important for at-risk learners who need to understand the purpose of learning and who need to maintain a sense of competence and self-control before, during, and after the lesson. Repeatedly, children lose their self-control when they reach their frustration levels and lose their sense of competence and purpose. This may be due to the difficulty of the material, thus leading to the inability to comprehend it.

The Directed Reading as Thinking Activities (DR-TA)

The directed reading as thinking activity, developed by Stauffer (1969), can be used in any subject area and is designed for group comprehension instruction (small or large groups). This approach is widely used by teachers because of its emphasis on developing higher-level thinking, and it is an easy strategy to use with children's stories or book chapters. This strategy involves the interchange of children's ideas and opinions and active comprehension stimulated by higher-level thinking questions.

A teacher's instructional strategies include designing lessons that aim to foster a sense of competence, self-control, and purpose.

The goals of the DR-TA include helping learners set a purpose for reading the material, making predictions using their background knowledge, synthesizing information directed by their purposes, verifying and revising their predictions as they read, and reaching their own conclusions about the story or text. There are two key phases of the DR-TA; the first is directing and guiding your students' thinking processes throughout the story or book chapter. The second involves extension and follow-up activities based on students' needs that were identified in the first phase. There is a variety of skills that can be addressed throughout the activity, which range from ideas synthesis through conceptual story mapping to emphasis on word-analysis skills.

This instructional strategy works best in a learning environment that encourages and values thinking and risk taking. Hopefully, you have created a sense of trust that encourages students to form hypotheses and predictions about the story or the activity. Within the group dynamic, students should feel comfortable to make predictions and have the opportunity to connect predictions to the story content. You will find a wide range of predictions that make it more interesting, and your at-risk learners should become engaged in making the story predictions since there are no right or wrong answers. Throughout this activity your students will be actively thinking.

The First Phase of the DR-TA

The first phase of the DR-TA involves a three-step cycle: first, making predictions using text information and personal background knowledge; second, reading to verify or alter predictions based on new text information and background knowledge; and third, providing support and proof of predictions based on text and personal knowledge (Ruddell and Ruddell, 1994).

I will use the literature selection of *Henry Huggins* by Beverly Cleary (1950) to illustrate the steps in the DR-TA in a small-group setting. The discussion between the teacher (T) and the students (S) will follow the steps of the DR-TA activity.

Receiving strategy is used with these divergent responses followed by refocusing on the reading purpose.

T: Please read the title and look at the picture on the cover and make predictions on what the story will be about. (This focusing question at the interpretive thinking level is designed to encourage predicting outcomes by activating personal background knowledge and to stimulate story predictions in the group.)

S1: It is about a boy named Henry Huggins.

S2: I think it might be about the trouble he gets into.

(Each student should make a prediction.)

T: These are all very interesting predictions. Now, let's read the first page of the story to find out what happens. (Receiving strategy is used with these divergent responses, followed by refocusing on the reading purpose. Students silently or orally read the first page and stop.)

T: What do you think now? (extending, interpretive level, predicting outcomes)

S1: It's about a boy named Henry Huggins and the dog that he finds.

S2: He names his dog Ribsy because he is very thin, and he wants to take him home.

T: Why do you think that? (extending)

S2: Because he likes him.

S1: Yeah, he wants to take him home and keep him.

T: Do you think Henry will be able to keep Ribsy?

S1: Yeah.

S2: Yeah.

T: Well, let's read a little more to find out.

The teacher continues the same pattern of predicting, discussing, verification, and proof throughout the chapter or the specified amount of pages to be read. After the students reach the end, a discussion occurs about verifying their predictions and proving them and then making new ones based on the new knowledge they acquire as they read.

The Second Phase of the DR-TA

The second phase of the DR-TA strategy, following the direct reading and discussion phase, is a follow-up extension activity. This should be decided based on your observations from the discussion. The activity can be on vocabulary development, group mapping, math, writing, or a variety of other areas. In the following activity, Think About It, students will be applying mathematical concepts and ideas that relate to the story about Henry Huggins. This is a superior way to integrate language arts and math after an engaging directed-reading-as-thinking activity.

Think About It

1. "Jeepers!" said Henry. "All of that for seventy-nine cents!"(page 33)

   A. Henry paid Mr. Pennycuff one silver dollar for the fish. How much change did Henry receive?

   B. If Henry had bought three bowls of fish, how much more money would he have needed?

2. "...I need to catch one thousand three hundred and thirty-one (worms) altogether." (page 75)

   A. Henry needed $14.36 to buy a football. Mr. Grumbie paid him one cent for each worm he caught. How much money did Henry already have?

   B. If Mr. Grumbie paid him two cents for each worm he caught, how much money would Henry make?

3. "At the pet store, they stopped to buy two pounds of horse meat from Mr. Pennycuff." (page 30)

   A. Henry bought Ribsy two pounds of horse meat every Friday. How many pounds of meat did he buy in one year?

   B. If the horse meat costs $2.00 a pound, how much money would Henry spend in a year?

4. "When Henry woke up one Monday morning in spring, the first thing he thought was, "Five more days until Saturday." On Tuesday the first thing he thought was, "Four more days until Saturday." (page 108)

   A. If it was Monday and the dog show was on a Saturday two weeks away, how many days would Henry have to wait?

   B. If it was Monday and the dog show was on a Saturday four weeks away, how many days would Henry have to wait?

5. "...Henry went to his room to watch his guppies. This time he counted thirty-eight babies." (page 41)

   A. At first, Henry had two guppies. If each pair of the thirty-eight guppies had thirty-eight babies, how many new guppies would there be?

   B. If Mr. Pennycuff paid Henry three cents for each of his 38 guppies, how much money would he have?

Reprinted from TCM 457 Favorite Authors: Beverly Cleary, *Teacher Created Materials, 1994*

Directed Listening-Thinking Activity (DL-TA)

Similar to the DR-TA, the directed-listening-as-thinking activity is an excellent strategy for developing sense of story plot through predictions and inferences (Stauffer, 1969). This is a wonderful strategy to use with younger students who cannot read just yet or even with older students to create suspense. In this strategy, the teacher reads a story to the class, stopping at planned points to ask for predictions. Make sure you have read the story beforehand, so you know where the good points are to stop. For older students you are trying to create suspense, so you do not want to ruin it by not stopping in time for obvious reasons. The typical stop points usually occur after the title, after the story introduction (about 1–2 paragraphs), at one or two points of high interest or suspenseful points, and just before the story ends.

As you read the story, you ask the students what they think the story will be about, why they think so, and what will happen next. At the final stop point, you will ask how the story will end. These are deliberately open-ended questions to give the students freedom to answer in their own ways. These questions will, hopefully, spark discussion, which invites students to offer their own interpretations.

It is very important that you accept your students' predictions and interpretations as long as they have some logical justification.

It is very important that you accept your students' predictions and interpretations as long as they have some logical justification. In the beginning, the responses may be very broad, but as the story plot develops, the answers should become more focused. As new information is provided to the students, they will refine their predictions and interpretations, which will help them to draw inferences and conclusions.

The DL-TA instructional strategy is very valuable for developing inferences and predictions about story events and outcomes and can easily and should most definitely be used as a springboard for extension activities. For example, the students may choose favorite characters and draw pictures of the characters in other settings. Some students may choose to illustrate different parts of the book and give it a new title. Some other students may assume the roles of different characters and act out the story as you narrate. There are many other options that can follow the DL-TA activity.

The Question-Answer Relationship Strategy (QAR)

The Question-Answer Relationship (QAR) strategy (Raphael, 1982, 1986) can be effectively used with students in grades one through six. This strategy helps students understand the thinking demands of questions and learn how to use information sources in response to the questions.

This instructional strategy classifies questions into four categories of information: right there, think and search, author and you, on my own. In brief, right there is information that is stated explicitly in the text and requires recall of information at the factual level of thinking. The second information source, think and search, is information that must be inferred or concluded from factual statements. The third information source is author and you, which is based on the combination of the student's personal knowledge and the information from the text. The final and fourth source, on my own, relies heavily on the student's background knowledge. This strategy is designed to help students understand and analyze the thinking demands of questions and the procedures required in developing answers. Students are faced with questions about expository texts in all of their classes, math, social studies, science, and language arts; thus, it is important for them to be able to differentiate between the kinds of questions and formulate appropriate answers. Often, at-risk learners are bombarded with questions, and they just give the same answer instead of thinking about what the question is asking. If they are aware of these four categories of information, it will help them in answering the many questions they face in their classes.

The purposes of the ReQuest strategy is to develop your student's active comprehension.

This strategy should be implemented over a four-day period and not in just one day. It is helpful if you tell your students what type of question you are asking, such as, "That's a think and search question." By doing this, it can alleviate fear and intrepidation that usually occurs when the student is unsure of the answer to the question.

Reciprocal Questioning (ReQuest)

The purposes of the ReQuest strategy is to develop your students' active comprehension. Through these strategies, students learn how to ask questions, set purposes, and synthesize information, which is required in all of the content areas. This strategy can serve to improve students' ability to self-monitor their comprehension processes and can be effective with a large group, a small group, or individual students.

The reciprocal questioning strategy, designed by Anthony Manzo (1969; Manzo & Manzo, 1990), is extremely valuable for developing students' ability to build comprehension, self-monitor responses, and create questions. In this strategy, the teacher and student take turns asking questions about a passage. You serve as a model for questioning, guiding them toward formulating a purpose for the question. The ReQuest strategy can be used effectively across the curriculum and in all grade levels. To effectively implement this strategy, begin by making sure the students have a copy of the story or content area reading material and follow the seven steps.

The first step is the introduction, which requires you to explain how this strategy works. It might be fun if you approach this as a game, especially for your at-risk learner; it can break down barriers and create a positive attitude.

The second step is the initial reading and student questioning; this is when everyone reads the first paragraph silently and then takes turns asking questions, beginning with the students asking the first round of questions. Students answering the questions must have their books closed.

In the third step of teacher questioning and modeling, it is your turn to ask your students the questions about the first paragraph. In this step you are modeling to your students how to ask questions and connect them to the answers that are provided. It is important to stress to your students that each question should be answered, and even "I don't know" responses must be supported. If you or your students are unsure of the answer, you must explain why.

> It might be fun if you approach this as a game, especially for your at-risk learner; it can break down barriers and create a positive attitude.

The fourth step is just a continuation of the previous step, to continue the reciprocal questioning as you progress through the text. You should demonstrate how the information in this segment connects to the information in the previous segment. Remember, you are modeling for your students how to logically ask questions and develop comprehension skills.

In the fifth step you are setting a purpose for reading by continued reading until you have enough information to begin predicting the outcome. Once you and your students have made predictions, turn them into questions. It is wise to record these predictions on the blackboard or, perhaps, on chart paper so you can return to them as you gain more information. Do not change any of the predictions or questions; record them verbatim. Remind students that sometimes not all of their questions are answered by the end of the story, but they may be answered through a discussion later on.

The sixth step is short but very important, silent reading. You should read to the end of the text or chapter to see if your predictions are correct.

The seventh and final step in this strategy is the follow-up discussion where you can address the purpose-setting question as well as some other questions that arise towards the end. It is important to show your students that there is a logic to reading, and it is important to devise the purpose-setting question. If the story did not answer all of your questions, this is the time to discuss it.

After your students learn how to use this ReQuest strategy, they can work in pairs or small groups to ask questions, predict outcomes, and provide explanations. Do not forget that you are modeling how to ask questions and what kinds of questions to ask, and you want to encourage your students to ask similar types of questions, not just factual recall ones.

Reciprocal Teaching

Much like the ReQuest strategy, reciprocal teaching uses teacher modeling to help students formulate questions and make predictions. This strategy is designed to develop students' comprehension and their comprehension monitoring ability. Included in this strategy are the following four skill processes—predicting, question generation, clarifying, and summarizing. Do these sound familiar? Yes, they are similar skill processes found in most of the strategies already described. The difference in reciprocal teaching is that halfway through the strategy, the student assumes the role of the teacher and is responsible for generating the questions from the group of students, clarifying predictions, and summarizing the reading section. While leading the discussion, the student must provide feedback and answer the questions. There are many ways this strategy can be used in your classroom, such as peer tutoring, cross-age reading and writing buddies, and cooperative learning. At-risk learners should be able to use this strategy; if not, perhaps, they can work in partners to lead the discussion. Either way, it is an empowering experience.

Since both of these strategies can be effective in all grade levels across the curriculum, this is a good chance to integrate reading and writing with another subject, such as science. In the example of the literature selection, *The Very Hungry Caterpillar* by Eric Carle (1969), a picture book about the metamorphosis of the butterfly, either the ReQuest or reciprocal teaching strategy can be tried out with your students. As a follow-up activity, the Life Cycle of a Butterfly activity can be used to discuss what happens to a caterpillar when it becomes a butterfly, like the caterpillar in the story. You can extend this activity for a higher grade level and have your students further research this phenomenon of nature and explain it to the class.

> Much like the ReQuest strategy, reciprocal teaching uses teacher modeling to help students formulate questions and make predictions.

Life Cycle of a Butterfly

Name_____

Directions: Color, cut, and glue in the correct section.

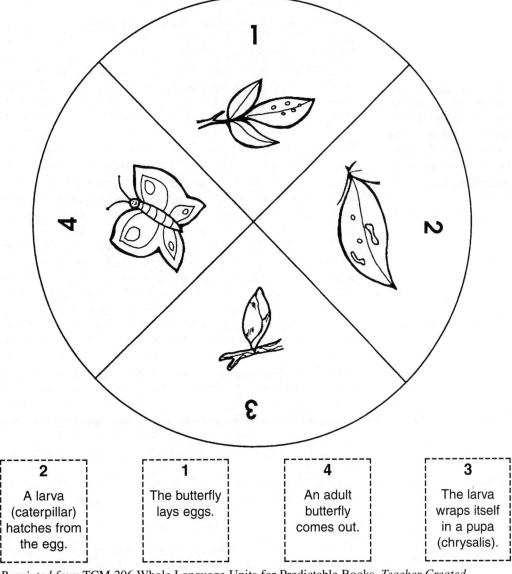

<table>
<tr><td>

2

A larva
(caterpillar)
hatches from
the egg.

</td><td>

1

The butterfly
lays eggs.

</td><td>

4

An adult
butterfly
comes out.

</td><td>

3

The larva
wraps itself
in a pupa
(chrysalis).

</td></tr>
</table>

Reprinted from TCM 206 Whole Language Units for Predictable Books, *Teacher Created Materials, 1995*

Vocabulary Self-Collection Strategy (VSS)

The vocabulary self-collection strategy (VSS) (Haggard, 1982, 1986; Ruddell, 1993) is intended to foster long-term acquisition and development of vocabulary. This strategy has two major characteristics: first of all, it focuses on words students want to learn and need to know, words that are important to them, and it stimulates word learning that usually occurs naturally; however, for at-risk learners, it is a struggle.

To begin using the vocabulary self-collection strategy after reading a chapter or discussing a unit, you ask the students to each nominate one word or term that they would like to know more about and add it to the class vocabulary list. You also nominate a word. Then, the students are required to tell you where they found their words, what they think the words mean in this context, and why they think the class should learn them.

During this discussion, students will bring in their background knowledge and prior experiences to come up with meanings.

This strategy works most effectively when the students are in small groups, each group nominates two words for the pool, and you also nominate two words for the pool. Give your students a few minutes to look back through the text to choose their words and then list them on the board or a piece of chart paper. As soon as the groups are ready, a representative from each group tells which words were chosen, where they were found, what the group believes they mean, and why they were chosen. As you write the words down, lead the discussion to define the word; begin with the context that was given to any other references in the classroom. Other students can participate in this discussion, contributing their opinions about the meaning of the word. During this discussion, students will bring in their background knowledge and prior experiences to come up with meanings.

After all of the nominated words have been discussed, a final class list is established by eliminating any words the class feels they already know or any duplicate words or terms. It is then up to you to choose the most appropriate words to add to the final class list. The chosen words are circled or highlighted and redefined so every student is clear about their definitions. These definitions can be written in vocabulary journals or any other lesson documents. The words that are not chosen by the class can be recorded by some students who wish to keep them in their own personal writing journals or vocabulary lists.

A follow-up activity for VSS requires the students to use the words in meaningful ways, to create connections between the new words and previously known words, encourages higher-level thinking, leads students to many other resources, and highlights the social nature of learning and language interaction. To encourage long-term retention of these words, some other follow-up activities may include a bulletin board Word of the Week, writing stories using some of the new words, or drawing pictures that help define the new words. The Interactive Cloze activities are always fun with new words and terms. This begins with a short passage that has some words deleted, but the first and last sentences are complete. Students can work individually or in pairs to complete the passage, and then upon completion they can compare their responses with a friend.   This activity highlights the importance of context clues and negotiating the correct meanings of the words.

This vocabulary strategy can make word learning fun and entertaining because it allows students to talk about and play with words, and they have the control over their own learning by choosing which words they want to nominate and ultimately choose for the final class list. VSS is a great activity for students to challenge themselves and their classmates by discovering new words, sounds, and definitions. At-risk learners will enjoy this activity because there is freedom and choice involved, and they have a chance to hear other students admit that they do not know everything, which can be comforting.

VSS is a great activity for students to challenge themselves and their classmates by discovering new words, sounds, and definitions.

On the following pages, a sample is provided for you to do a vocabulary self-collection with your class and a follow-up Interactive Cloze activity. The passage Olympians Don't Quit, comes from a curriculum guide *Share the Olympic Dream*, written by Teacher Created Materials, and provided by the United States Olympic Committee. The passage can be read by your whole class or a small group and enjoyed by your students, especially since most children watch the Olympics because there are competitors from around the world, which makes it very exciting. From this passage, the students will nominate their new vocabulary words and then complete the follow-up activity, using the new vocabulary words. It is topics like sports that are stimulating to many children, especially at-risk learners, because sports have a unique appeal; although they are competitive; they can still be fun.

Olympians Don't Quit

Do you ever want to give up because something happened that made your goal harder to achieve? It has happened to Olympians, too.

Dutch athlete Fanny Blankers-Koen, age 22, was looking forward to the 1940 Olympic Games, certain she would win the gold as a sprinter. But, World War II came along, and both the 1940 and the 1944 Olympic Games were canceled. She continued training, gave birth to a son and daughter, and looked forward to the 1948 Games. By the time Fanny was 30, she was much older than the other sprinters. She won the 100-meter dash and the 80-meter hurdles, only to be mobbed by reporters who would not let her rest for her remaining events. Yet, she went on to win the 200-meter race and was a member of the 4 x 100-meter relay team. Fanny was the first woman ever to have won four track and field gold medals in the same Olympic Games.

In 1938, army sergeant Karoly Takacs was a member of his national pistol shooting team and expected to win in the 1940 Games. But, a tragic accident happened. While he was on a maneuver a hand grenade exploded, leaving Karoly without his right hand. His hopes for gold dashed, Takacs was allowed to remain in the army despite his disability. He was severely depressed, but he began training again with a pistol, this time using his left hand. At the 1948 Olympic Games, Captain Takacs stood on the winner's platform, wearing his gold medal for pistol shooting. He won it with his left hand, the hand he had never used for shooting prior to the accident 10 years earlier.

Ray Ewry of Layfayette, Indiana, spent much time of his childhood in a wheelchair. Doctors believed that he would never walk again. Yet, he devoted hours to exercises and not only walked, but he developed great strength in his legs. He won three of the track and field jumping events at Paris in 1900, repeated at St. Louis in 1904, and once again swept the jumping events at the 1908 Olympic Games in London.

When Wilma Rudoph was four, she caught scarlet fever and pneumonia. It was thought she would never walk again. Yet her mother drove her long distances to therapy, and her brothers and sisters spent many hours massaging her useless legs. By age six she was walking in special shoes, but Wilma did not stop there. In high school she starred in basketball. Switching to track, she made the U.S. Olympic Team in 1956 and won two bronze medals. In 1960, she returned from the Games with three gold medals. She was a winner personally, too, being one of the most popular athletes of all time.

Olympians Don't Quit *(cont.)*

Like most boys growing up in Flint, Michigan, trying out for Little League was an important part of the life for young Jim Abbott. The fact that he did not have a right hand made no difference. At an early age, he had learned to pitch and bat left-handed. When catching a ball in the field, he wore the glove on his left hand, quickly switching it to his right as he threw the runners out. At the University of Michigan, Jim pitched his way to many honors, including the Big Ten Player of the Year. As a member of the 1988 U.S. Olympic Team, he made two appearances on the mound. In the final game against Japan, he pitched a complete game to clinch the gold medal for the USA. He was no longer thought of as a player with one hand. Although he had reached his life-time goal of earning an Olympic gold medal, he continued his athletic career by pitching in professional major league baseball.

Directions to student: Retell the stories of these great athletes.

_____ pitcher Jim_____ led his team at the University of _____ and was named outstanding player in the _____. He pitched his USA team to victory in the 1988 Games.

_____ Rudolph showed her family and friends that indeed she would _____ again. She starred in high school _____ and went out for _____. She won two Olympic _____ medals in 1956 and returned to win _____ gold medals in 1960.

Ray _____ left his _____ and exercised to develop great _____ strength. He became an outstanding jumper and swept those events in the _____ Games of 1900 and repeated in the following Olympic Games at _____ and_____.

_____ Blankers-Koen missed two Olympic Games because of _____. In 1948 at age ____ she became the first woman to win four _____ and _____ events.

In 1938 Karoly _____ looked forward to winning the gold medal in _____ shooting. In a tragic accident he lost his _____ hand. Rather than give up his sport, he taught himself to _____ with his left hand, and in the 1948 Olympic Games he stood on the _____ with a _____ medal around his neck.

Reprinted from TCM 064 Share the Olympic Dream, *Teacher Created Materials, 1995*

Reading Response Groups

Another instructional strategy a teacher can use in the creation of an engaging literacy community is the formation of reading response groups. In these groups, students discuss their responses and construct their own personal meanings from a text, based on prior knowledge and the new knowledge gained from the text. Depending on the genre of the text and the chosen stance, teachers can enhance the goal of providing students with pleasurable experiences with various literature, including historical novels and science fiction pieces, or even mathematical word problems. When you set up these response groups, you must be prepared to expect, respect, and accept a variety of student responses since you are encouraging students to voice their opinions and share ideas. Ultimately, you should aim to create a community of learners within the classroom, which encourages students' personal responses and helps the students to develop ownership, pride, self-respect, and a love of learning. Both students and teachers alike become members of this literacy community which grows and develops.

You should supply prompts which will guide the students to think beyond the limits of the text and which will raise some curiosity.

The key to the success of reading response groups is to have well-constructed and well-communicated task goals so the students know what they are supposed to be doing and do not go off task too often. Since you are giving them freedom to respond, you must accept that there may be some extraneous talking, but if you plan the task goals and the time allotment proportionally, there should not be any problems. You should supply prompts which will guide the students to think beyond the limits of the text and which will raise some curiosity.

Reading response groups can begin in small groups of 5–6 students and then open up to the large class response. Afterward, have students reflect on the response group process for future activities.

The need for teachers to interact with the students in a social way through the instructional strategies is considerable, especially during response groups. You want to teach your students how to be independent learners by guiding them through the process and helping them become responsible for monitoring their own learning rather than relying on external monitors, such as you, their teacher. If you truly want to help students become self-regulated and develop positive attitudes that lead to success, you can do so by adding statements to lesson discussions about students being in control of their own learning (Pearson, 1991) while at the same time modeling and helping students learn to be in control of their learning.

You can also be a good role model for your students by participating in reading response groups or expressing your love for learning. During sustained silent reading (SSR), go ahead and take out your book to read. This shows the students that reading can be pleasurable and that you do, in fact, like to learn. Also, when you introduce the ideas and initiate literacy activities, you are promoting positive attitudes toward learning. Other literate role models such as parents and community members can participate as well.

Reader's Theater

Reader's theater is an activity which encourages students to bring characters to life and sparks enthusiasm throughout the class. It can be done with a variety of materials, for example, a literature selection or a chapter out of a history book. Students are not dramatizing the story or passage, rather they use their own voices and facial expressions to bring the characters to life through dramatic play form and minimal actions. Reader's theater provides a wonderful opportunity for your students to develop an understanding of characterization, setting, plot, and story resolution. The script is altered so there is a narrator who reads the descriptive parts, and the readers or actors speak the characters' parts. Therefore, the students have a chance to become part of the script and offer their own interpretations of the passage. Although this strategy works most effectively with older students, it can also be done with younger students, using familiar stories or fairy tales.

> Reader's theater is an activity which encourages students to bring characters to life and sparks enthusiasm throughout the class.

When you introduce reader's theater, explain that the readers/actors will sit in a circle and read the script without costumes, props, or actions. Encourage your students to think of stories or content area passages that contain interesting characters, lots of dialogue, a story plot with suspense, and a special or surprise ending. Some ideas for the primary grades are storybooks such as *Miss Nelson Is Missing!* (Allard & Marshall, 1977), *The Cat in the Hat* (Dr. Seuss, 1987), and *Jack in the Beanstalk* (Howe, 1989). At the upper primary and intermediate grades, possible selections may be *Why Mosquitoes Buzz in People's Ears* (Aardema, 1975), Chapter 6 from *Runaway to Freedom* (Smucker, 1979), or *Annie and the Old One* (Miles, 1971).

It is really fun for the students to choose which parts they want to read, and this can be negotiated in small groups or in the whole-class setting. Designate an area in your room that can be used as a stage, preferably the rug area, where there is enough space to move around if needed. Before you begin, ask the readers/actors to read over their parts silently. Then, have the actors read out loud to practice voice intonation and expression to convey feelings, emotions, and moods. The rest of the class will be the audience. It is essential to remind the audience they need to use their imaginations to help create the characters and the settings. After the performance, the students can switch roles or alter the script in some other way. You can discuss how the roles were portrayed, how the script can be altered or modified, and the audience's reactions.

Reader's theater is only one of many reading aloud activities students love to participate in. Other such activities include shared group reading, partner reading (with a friend, with the teacher, or with a role model), younger or older reading buddies, choral reading, or echo reading. All of these experiences can be meaningful literacy tasks when the students have the choice of the reading material and the choice of the activity. The reading material can be from any content area they choose, not only from language arts class. Reading aloud activities can improve oral language and listening skills, build vocabulary, aid reading comprehension, motivate students, and have a positive impact on students' attitudes toward reading. It is an easy component to incorporate into any reading and language, science, social studies, or math program at any grade level. Reading aloud can be a powerful technique for promoting story enjoyment and literature appreciation and for motivating students to read science and social studies texts. When given the chance to become an active participant or an actor, any literacy activity can be enjoyable to all students, especially your at-risk students who like to move around and talk. Let them do it through acting out a story or a chapter in a book. Most importantly, the activity should include motivational value for the students, which is just as important as the material chosen for the activity.

Most importantly, the activity should include motivational value for the students, which is just as important as the material chosen for the activity.

A Final Note on Instructional Strategies
Many of these strategies should be nongraded activities that infuse motivational characteristics into the learning environment which will promote learning in a nonintimidating, friendly, comforting, and entertaining way. The literacy activities provided must be engaging and maintain moderate difficulty which promotes student interest and involvement but does not promote frustration, especially for at-risk learners. When you are planning these activities, it is important to remember that allowing your students to choose the material which is of interest to them is a powerful motivator. The choices must be interesting to the students, or else there will be no motivation to engage in them; in order for students to become engaged, a sense of ownership is needed. To be most effective, you want to use this knowledge on a regular basis when you are planning your lessons and using your many instructional strategies to convey your message.

Assessment Practices

In previous chapters, we have covered motivational theories, personal and cognitive influences, creating a positive learning environment, and instructional strategies to use in your classroom and share with parents. Before we close the book on motivation, we need to discuss assessment of your at-risk students. Since many of them possess a great fear of tests, we need to use alternative methods of assessment in all of the subject areas. These can range from portfolios, inventories, surveys, anecdotal records, observations, logs, journals, miscue analysis, student self-evaluations, checklists, and rubrics. Authentic assessment is the process of gathering evidence and documenting students' learning and growth in an authentic context (Ryan, 1994). All of these forms of authentic assessment help us examine the teaching and learning process in a meaningful way by focusing on the process as much as the product.

The use of portfolios as a form of assessment across the curriculum has risen in recent years, as well as have the other forms of assessment. One reason for this might be because authentic assessment focuses on high-level literacy abilities, using authentic or real life literacy tasks that are needed in the community or will be required in the workplaces in the next century. Another reason might be because the portfolios are able to link assessment with instruction much better than other kinds of tests and reflect the entire learning process, as opposed to testing a specific skill in a specific way on a specific day, such as in traditional standardized testing. Whatever the reason, the fact that portfolios offer many benefits to both students and teachers cannot be disputed; therefore, the reform movement for authentic assessment has surged ahead.

The portfolio is a tool for expanding the quantity and quality of information used to examine literacy learning and to plan for instruction.

The portfolio is a tool for expanding the quantity and quality of information used to examine literacy learning and to plan for instruction. Through the use of portfolios, students are encouraged to become active participants and evaluators of their own learning. These are some of the reasons why teachers would rather use portfolios as a single form of assessment or in addition to tests to give a broader picture of the student. "A portfolio is a cultural artifact, a highly individualized artifact, intended to serve the needs of a particular class working with a particular instructor" (Metzger and Bryant, 1994, p. 5). Thus, a portfolio offers much more information about the student to a teacher than the results from a traditional standardized test. Portfolios are giving teachers the power and authority to assess students' accomplishments that they once had before the invasion of traditional standardized tests.

Rubric-Based and Assigned-Task Assessment

Rubric-based assessment answers the questions of how, what, when, and why when grading writing samples or open-ended math problems that potentially have more than one solution. This kind of math problem encourages the student to think about the mathematical concepts rather than getting the right answer. The use of the rubric assessment allows you to grade an open-ended math problem so that you focus on the process the student went through to arrive at the answer as opposed to the answer he/she arrived at. Rubrics make the teacher's expectations public knowledge, which will really help at-risk learners.

For assessing writing pieces, there are two types of rubrics that are used: holistic and analytic The holistic rubric is used to evaluate the whole piece of writing. The analytic rubric includes score points which are assigned to different elements that should be looked at in a piece of writing. These kinds of rubrics are totally quantitative; the numbers tell the story. Both kinds of rubrics can be used in two ways, as a teaching tool and as an assessment device. Rubrics can be developed by teachers or students as part of the writing process. The sample of a writing assessment rubric on the next page is helpful to both teachers and students because the expectations for each score is very clear. Rubrics can be changed according to the subject matter and the type of assignment.

Writing Assessment Rubric

Score 3: High Pass
- Student responds to prompt.
- Student writes in complete sentences.
- Student uses mainly conventional spelling.
- Story is in proper sequence.

Score 2: Pass
- Student responds to prompt.
- Student expresses complete thoughts but not necessarily complete sentences.
- Student uses some invented spelling, but it does not inhibit understanding.
- Student may not tell events in the proper sequence.

Score 1: Needs Revision
- Student may not respond to prompt.
- Student expresses self in a way that inhibits understanding.
- Student does not demonstrate knowledge of sound/symbol relationships.
- Student does not tell the story in the proper sequence.

Score 0: No Response

Reprinted from TCM 777 Language Arts Assessment 3–4, *Teacher Created Materials, 1994*

Checklists are a form of assigned-task assessment which are included in other methods of assessment. It is simply a list of tasks to be observed by the observer during an activity or a performance of knowledge. When you make up a checklist for a lesson or unit, think about the most important tasks that need to be accomplished in order to reach the end goal. You are looking for evidence that knowledge has been acquired and that students show a level of competence in that particular task.

Your checklist can be very general or very specific, depending on the goal of the lesson or unit.

Concluding Remarks

These three forms of assessment are especially helpful in assessing at-risk learners because they account for different styles of learning. Often at-risk learners will not do well on traditional tests, and, unfortunately, they are penalized for that. Using alternative forms of assessment allows your at-risk learners to show competence and acquisition of knowledge in nontraditional ways. Also, these forms of assessment invite the learner to open up their portfolios and reflect on their learning process. They are able to see growth and progress in many areas instead of looking at just one number. This is a more comforting thought for these learners. Most importantly, portfolios give learners a sense of ownership which makes them feel proud of their efforts.

Some Final Thoughts

Meeting the Challenge of At-Risk Learners

Motivating at-risk students is one of the biggest challenges you will face as a teacher. The most important aspects you must remember is that these learners really and truly want to learn; unfortunately, they have had negative experiences and felt frustration too many times. However, by identifying the personal and cognitive factors that influence these learners, you are one step closer to successfully teaching them and helping them achieve to their fullest potential.

Throughout this book, I have taken a social constructivist perspective of understanding and learning, which addresses the social domain of the classroom and the interpersonal and intrapersonal elements of the student. The teacher creates a learning environment that provides motivational opportunities that foster intentions to read, and the students are involved in engaging literacy activities that require active comprehension and construction of meaning. This environment emphasizes motivation, positive attitudes, social interaction, purposeful dialogue, negotiated meaning, understanding, and the development of the learner's intention to learn.

> Motivating at-risk students is one of the biggest challenges you will face as a teacher.

Motivation is a complex concept that affects all of us, and by knowing the internal and external motivating factors, we can begin to chip away at this iceberg. The motivational theories were offered to give you a foundation to build on so you can identify the reasons why students are unmotivated to participate in a particular activity. You need to ask yourself the following questions: Are they afraid of failure or success? Do they not understand and are embarrassed? These questions can be answered with the help of these motivational theories. There is always a reason behind the lack of motivation; you just have to do some investigating to figure out the answer.

The instructional strategies that were offered can be tried out in your classrooms and shared with parents who can try them out at home. They can be used in all of the content areas and carry over to music, art, and physical education, as well. And, finally, since we need to assess and evaluate both the learners and ourselves, alternative forms of assessment are discussed. These methods help us evaluate if our students are learning what we want them to learn and if we are teaching them the best that we can. Reflection is a key element in the learning process. It allows us to look inside and see what is going on. Reflection entails judgment, as we need to judge our growth and development. Without reflection on it, we have no way of knowing where we have been and where we are going. There are important answers to search for and questions to continue to ask ourselves as we journey through the learning process with our students.

> **The instructional strategies that were offered can be tried out in your classrooms and shared with parents to try them out at home.**

It is worth repeating that at-risk learners want to learn and achieve success; it just takes them a little longer to reach their goals. We have the ability to assist them on their road to achievement, which is a comforting thought. These students turn to us for the guidance and encouragement which we need to give each and every day in our classrooms. It is up to us to create that positive, warm, and inviting learning environment within the perimeters we are given.

The development of intrinsic motivation is a goal each learner strives for while journeying through the learning process. The development of this kind of motivation takes time and happens differently for each learner. On the one hand, high-interest/high-achieving learners probably have intrinsic motivation. This may be a result of positive experiences with some of the extrinsic motivators, such as good grades, positive feedback from the teacher, enough time to complete activities successfully, and satisfaction brought on by a high level of comprehension. On the other hand, low-interest/low-achieving learners who are at risk of failing, unfortunately, have not developed intrinsic motivation, which may be a result of negative experiences with some of the extrinsic motivations in the classroom, such as poor grades, unfinished activities due to time restrictions, negative feedback from teachers or peers, and a low level of comprehension, thus leading to low self-esteem and self-worth. In light of this knowledge, it is very important that at-risk learners develop the intrinsic motivations to be successful within the classroom learning environment.

There are many implications for teachers that derive from this discussion; specifically, the external factors in the classroom can provide many motivational opportunities and promote intentions to learn which can be internalized. The classroom environment and the teacher must provide activities that are meaningful literacy tasks which enhance children's learning and go beyond learners' interactions with texts. These kinds of literacy activities enable students to engage in meaningful, interesting tasks, allowing students to construct their own knowledge based on prior knowledge. Some examples of these activities can be math quiz partners, reading aloud, role playing, reader's theater, or group science experiments. Through these activities, students can recognize the value of learning and raise their interest and potential as learners and thinkers. The classroom environment must also promote an inviting atmosphere where children help each other enjoy reading, writing, acting, drawing, and discovering and where they share their enthusiasm and knowledge through language interaction.

Remember when you are working with at-risk learners to view the world through their eyes and think of how you can avoid frustration for them.

Remember when you are working with at-risk learners to view the world through their eyes and think of how you can avoid frustration for them. By motivating them to become active in their own learning process and giving them support and encouragement, you are making their lives easier. You are empowering them with hope, which can go a long way and make a lasting difference.

References

Aardema, V. (1975). <u>Why mosquitoes buzz in people's ears.</u> New York: Puffin.

Allard, H., & Marshall, J. (1977). <u>Miss Nelson is missing!</u> Boston: Houghton Mifflin.

Anderson, R. C., Wilson, P. T., & Fielding, L. G. (1985). <u>A new focus on free reading.</u> Symposium presentation at the National Reading Conference. San Diego, CA.

Applebee, A. N., Langer, J. A., & Mullis, V. S. (1988). <u>Who reads best? Factors related to reading achievement in grades 3, 7, and 11.</u> (Report #17-R-01). National Assessment of Educational Progress. Princeton, NJ: Education Testing Service.

Au, K. H. (1980). Participation structures in reading lessons: Analysis of a culturally appropriate instructional event. <u>Anthropology and Education Quarterly,</u> 11, 91–115.

Carle, E. (1969). <u>The very hungy caterpillar.</u> New York: Philomel Books.

Cleary, B. (1950). <u>Henry Huggins.</u> New York: Morrow & Co.

Covington, M. (1992). <u>Making the grade.</u> New York: Cambridge University Press.

Deci, E. L. (1975). <u>Intrinsic motivation.</u> New York: Plenum.

Dewey, J. (1938). <u>Experience and education.</u> New York: Macmillan.

Dyson, A. H. (1991). The word and the world: Reconceptualizing written language development, or do rainbows mean a lot to little girls? <u>Research in the Teaching of English,</u> 25, 97–123.

Ehri, L. C. (1991). Development of the ability to read words. In R. Barr, M. L. Kamil, P. Mosenthal, & P. D. Pearson (Eds.), <u>Handbook of reading research: Volume II</u> (pp. 383–417). White Plains, NY: Longman.

Guthrie, J. T. (1994, August/September). Creating interest in reading. <u>Reading Today,</u> 24.

Haggard, M. R. (1982). The vocabulary self-collection strategy: An active approach to word learning. <u>Journal of Reading,</u> 26, 203–207.

Haggard, M. R. (1986). The vocabulary self-collection strategy: Using student interest and world knowledge to enhance vocabulary growth. <u>Journal of Reading,</u> 29, 634–642.

Howe, J. (1989). <u>Jack and the beanstalk.</u> Boston: Little Brown and Co.

Hynds, S. (1990). Talking life and literature. In S. Hynds & D. L. Rubin (Eds.), <u>Perspectives on talk and learning.</u> Urbana, IL: National Council of Teachers of English.

Loban, W. D. (1963). <u>The language of elementary school children.</u> (NCTE Research Report No. 2). Champaign, IL: National Council of Teachers of English.

Manzo, A. V (1969). The ReQuest procedure. <u>Journal of Reading,</u> 13, 23–126.

Manzo, A. V., & Manzo U. (1990). <u>Content area reading: A heuristic approach.</u> Columbus, OH: Merrill.

Maslow, A. H. (1954). <u>Motivation and personality.</u> New York: Harper.

Mathewson, G. C. (1994) Model of attitude influence upon reading and learning to read. In R. B. Ruddell, M. R. Ruddell, & H. Singer (Eds.), <u>Theoretical models and processes of reading</u> (4th ed., p. 1131–1161). Newark, DE: International Reading Association.

McClelland, D. C., Atkinson, J. W., Clark, R. T., & Lowell, E. L. (1953). <u>The achievement motive.</u> New York: Appleton-Century-Crofts.

Metzger, E., & Bryant, L. (1994, Winter). Portfolio assessment: Pedagogy, power, and the student. <u>Portfolio News,</u> 5(2), 5–8.

Miles, M. (1971). <u>Annie and the old one</u>. Boston: Little Brown and Co.

Mullis, I. V. S., & Jenkins, L. B. (1990). <u>The reading report card, 1971–1988</u>. Princeton, NJ: Educational Testing Service.

Mullis, I. V. S., Campbell, J. R., & Farstrup, A. E. (1993) <u>NAEP 1992 Reading report card for the nation and the states</u>. Washington, D.C.: Office of Educational Research and Improvement.

Piaget J., & Inhelder, B. (1969). <u>The psychology of the child</u>. New York: Basic Books.

Pearson, P. D. (1991). Literacy and schooling. In R. Barr, M. L. Kamil, P. Mosenthal, & P. D. Pearson (Eds.), <u>Handbook of reading research: Volume II</u> (pp. 383–417). White Plains, NY: Longman.

Raphael, T. E. (1982). Question-answering strategies for children. <u>The Reading Teacher, 36</u>, 186–190.

Raphael, T. E. (1986). Teaching question-answer relationships, revisited. <u>The Reading Teacher, 39</u>, 516–523.

Riordan, M. E. (1992). <u>Athletes are readers, too!: A program to motivate children to read</u>. Unpublished master's thesis, University of California, Berkeley.

Rosenblatt, L. M. (1978). <u>The reader, the text, the poem: The transactional theory of the literary work</u>. Carbondale, IL: Southern Illinois University Press.

Rosenblatt, L. M. (1994). The transactional theory of reading and writing. In R.B. Ruddell, M.R. Ruddell, & H. Singer (Eds.), <u>Theoretical models and processes of reading</u> (4th ed., p. 1057–1092). Newark, DE: International Reading Association.

Ruddell, M. R. (1993). <u>Teaching content reading and writing</u>. Boston: Allyn & Bacon.

Ruddell, M. R., & Ruddell, R. B. (1994). Language acquisition and literacy processes. In R. B. Ruddell, M. R. Ruddell, & H. Singer (Eds.), <u>Theoretical models and processes of reading</u> (4th ed., p. 83–103). Newark, DE: International Reading Association.

Ruddell, R. B., & Unrau, N. (1994). Reading as a meaning construction process: The reader, the text, and the teacher. In R. B. Ruddell, M. R. Ruddell, & H. Singer (Eds.), <u>Theoretical models and processes of reading</u> (4th ed., p. 996–1056). Newark, DE: International Reading Association.

Ryan, C. D. (1994). <u>Authentic assessment</u>. Westminster, CA: Teacher Created Materials.

Seuss, Dr. (1987). <u>The cat in the hat</u>. New York: Random House.

Slavin, R. E. (1991). <u>Educational psychology</u> (3rd ed.). Englewood Cliffs, NJ: Prentice Hall.

Smucker, B. (1979). <u>Runaway to freedom</u>. New York: Harper Trophy.

Spaulding, C. L. (1992). The motivation to read and write. In J. W. Irwin & M. A. Doyle (Eds.), <u>Reading/writing connections: Learning from research</u> (p. 177–201). Newark, DE: International Reading Association.

Stauffer, R. G. (1969). <u>Directing reading maturity as a cognitive process</u>. New York: Harper & Row.

Vygotsky, L. S. (1978). <u>Mind in society: The development of higher psychological processes</u>. M. Cole, V. John-Steiner, S. Scribner, & E. Souberman (Eds.), Cambridge MA: Harvard University Press.

U.S. Government Accounting Office Report. (July, 1993). <u>Briefing report to the chairman, sub-committee on children, family drugs and alcoholism, committee on labor and human resources, U.S. Senate: Poor preschool-aged chldren: Numbers increase but most not in preschool</u>. Washington, DC: United States General Accounting Office.

White, E. B. (1952). <u>Charlotte's web</u>. New York: Harper & Row.

Mary Riordan Karlsson is currently pursuing her Doctorate in Education at the University of California, Berkeley where she received a Masters Degree in Language and Literacy. She has taught kindergarten through eighth grade in New York City and San Francisco and has worked extensively with at-risk students. She has also taught a freshman seminar on critical reading, writing, and study skills at UC Berkeley. Mary is a supervisor for a teacher education program and works with master teachers throughout the East Bay Area. Her professional interests include the affective influences on literacy development, specifically the areas of motivation and attitude, the social and cultural aspects of literacy events, and technology in the classroom. Mary and her husband live in Piedmont, California.

ISBN 1-55734-890-1
50999

9 781557 348906

Teacher Created Materials

Teacher Created Materials, Inc.
6421 Industry Way
Westminster, CA 92683

ISBN 1-55734-890-1

0 14467 00890 5